I remember him, that's the boy from Hainault

By James Martinson

To Barbara, thank you for being my wife.

To Paul for proofreading, revising and publishing.

To Jo Jolley, for all the trust you've had in me over the years. Believe me, I really did enjoy working for you.

And to my cousin George Hallahan and friend John Bellyou, who are no longer with us.

Prologue

It seems like yesterday I was an eight-year-old boy, playing out on the streets of Hainault where most people would have known me during the late 1940s and 50s as 'Jimmy'. Then a few years older, ducking and diving, trying to make a few bob from paper rounds and working in fairgrounds. I left school with no qualifications and my first job at fourteen was working in the Foreign Exchange. Then it was on to the Merchant Navy, the docks, being a milkman... then working at Tower Bridge and finally a self-employed painter and decorator.

This is a whirlwind tour of my life. Time has gone very fast for me and the only thing I regret was not having a camera with me all the time. Some of the situations I've been in have been very funny wouldn't have been out of place in a television sitcom. Now, neither rich nor poor, I live a comfortable life with my wife, in Essex.

Index

Epilogue

The Boy from Hainault

Chapter One

London's East End, 1945

I came into this world on 22nd January 1945. My mother was Ann Catherine Margaret Martinson (nee Gard) and my father, William Charles Martinson, known as Bill. My surname originates from the Martensens of Denmark, but my grandfather thought the original sounded too German so had it officially changed.

I was born in Dunbar House, Glengall Grove, Poplar. I shared this address with my older sisters, June and Rita. Dunbar House was a tenement block, housing around twenty families. Some of the buildings in our road were bombed during the war, as we were close to the Millwall Docks. The war ended on May 8th much to my family's relief.

My father worked as a boilermaker's labourer but shortly after the war, became a docker. To be honest I don't remember much about my infant years, apart from that we were all well looked after. My mother, like most women of that era was very house proud with what little they had. We had a flat, and a roof over our heads. Many people were knocked from pillar to post in the East End and I can't imagine half of what they must have gone through.

When I was about three years old, I was playing out in the street and fell down a bomb crater, hurting myself badly and leaving me with scarring under my chin. About this time my mother had another baby, and a younger sister for me called Linda. It was also time to move somewhere bigger, so my parents decided the destination would be Hainault.

Chapter Two

Hainault, 1949

We moved to 173 Huntsman Road in Hainault, a three-bedroomed house with a large kitchen, dining room and a bathroom. It also had a large back garden and smaller front garden. I imagine my parents were delighted!

If you don't know Hainault very well, let me tell you a little about it. In the mid-1930s, the London County Council as they were then known, began to plan one of its 'out country cottage estates' in the part of Hainault that was then a rural corner of the Chigwell urban district, but the project was delayed by the outbreak of war. The LCC acquired the land in 1943 and construction began four years later. Almost 2,800 homes were built during the next six years, together with a shopping centre on Manford Way. Roman Catholic and Anglican churches were also built as part of the communal amenities. Behind Huntsman Road there were fields I was looking forward to playing in and about a mile further on was Fairlop Aerodrome, that played an important role in the war. It was a surprise to learn that prisoners of war had built many of these houses. They were billeted in the area and many stayed in England after the war ended.

There was also a railway station taking you into the East End of London and beyond, and the vast Hainault Forest with its lake and golf course. Hainault was like another country for me. Wherever I looked there were open spaces, grass and fresh air, unlike where we'd come from in Millwall, with its poverty, enclosed spaces, docks and ships. Though little did I realise ships would become a significant part of my life in the future.

Manford Way Junior School was a fifteen-minute walk from our house so that's where my two older sisters went, often with me and Linda in tow. We had to pass a row of shops that were being built at that time but before long were up and running with flats above.

By now my father was working hard as a docker and we had a comfortable life. I remember my mum having a go at him for buying a motorbike to get to work as she thought it was dangerous. So, he didn't own one for long. I don't remember him doing much work in the house.

He saw himself as the breadwinner, and the rest of you could get on with it. He wouldn't even cut the grass in our new garden. So, my mum did the chores and other work, like painting and decorating.

Meanwhile my father found local friends who also worked in the Royal Group of Docks and managed to catch a lift to work every day. He liked that, especially now he didn't have a motorbike.

I was, I suppose, a street kid. Out finding friends and having a laugh, always on the go. Our back garden was about fifty feet long with a wicker fence at the end. Beyond that was a large field and a stream, then more fields and at the end of all that was the London Transport Social Club. If you kept walking you'd be on Forest Road, then left towards Fairlop Station. A right would bring you to Hog Hill, leading down to Hainault Industrial Estate. There were maybe fifty or more factories on the estate, bringing jobs for everyone but paying country rates so you were never going to get rich there.

I don't have a lot of memories from my infant school years at Manford Way, but I think I was a bit of a git towards the teachers, who in turn told the teachers at the Junior School what to look forward to.

Looking from our front room window across the road was another playing field and next to this, Kingswood Secondary School where my sister June had started going in the early fifties. Having three sisters at home with me did cause arguments now and again but on the whole things were okay.

My parents, like many others were quite strict. Evening meals meant all of us at the table, and you ate everything put in front of you. And you kept quiet unless spoken to. People always say their mum's cooking was the best and it was true that mums knew how to scrape up a meal when money wasn't flying about. My mother made a good bread pudding and we also loved her apple crumble. She also made honeycomb and slabs of toffee. Sunday mornings would always see me in the kitchen as meal time approached, and when mum cooked the cabbage and greens it was always me who ended up with the water they were boiled in. If it was roast lamb, then it was me that had the bone. I loved it. But roast beef was my favourite meal on a Sunday as I knew that on the Monday there would be a bowl of beef dripping in the larder and I was the only one who liked it. Fresh bread and dripping, with salt and pepper was something to die for.

Anyway, back to Manford Way Junior School. Our teachers in the fifties were Mrs Bird, Mr Neville, Mrs Lyons, Miss Kingwell and Mr Holland, to name a few. I don't know why but I just didn't like teachers. I was always polite to everyone outside of school but inside I was your typical cheeky chappie. Mrs Bird was in a wheelchair but used to whizz around the classroom like a formula one driver. It's a wonder she didn't have a pit stop in the corner of the room and must have had at least three tyre changes every year. One morning in class, I'd done something wrong and before I knew it she was at my side demanding I stand on a chair. She started to hit me on the legs with a ruler and it hurt so much that pooped my pants. She obviously noticed and took me out of the classroom, telling me to clean myself up and handing me a pair of blue elasticated knickers. I don't remember what happened when I got home that day, but I expect my mother would have agreed with the punishment. For her it was all about teachers doing their jobs properly.

When I was about eight years old, I was coming home from school one afternoon and noticed a car outside our house. It was a Vauxhall Wyvern. When I got inside my dad was sitting in his chair and asked if I liked our car. I replied that I did and that now we could go out. He said we could when he'd passed his driving test! Fortunately, it was only a few weeks before he passed, and we could go places. Our road was quite long, and we were only the third family to own a car. Nowadays it would be hard to park outside your own house in that street as there were no driveways and only small front gardens.

It became a regular thing for the family to visit my Dad's sister, Francis, in Canning Town. They had a four-bedroomed house in Rodgers Road, opposite the Ground Rent Tavern public house. My aunt lived there with her husband George and their sons, George and Jimmy. Also living there was my Grandmother. We usually had lunch and a short walk to Rathbone Market, a long lane of stalls selling all sorts. It was always a good afternoon out and our Grandmother gave us children two shillings and sixpence for the trip.

Back home I was out on the streets again. One thing I was good at was Knock Down Ginger. I'd knock on doors and run away, and it was all good, clean fun. Well it was for us. Winter months were the worst for playing outside, though I didn't mind the snow as there were always plenty of things you could do, like making a slide or rolling a snowball until it was the size of a boulder and leave it in the middle of the road. Well, I did say I was a bit of a git.

It was during the winter months I got a paper round. At the end of our road was Elmbridge Road and at the end of this was a prefab estate. At one end of the estate was a row of four shops. Bennetts, a newsagent; a general store and Bairds, the television repair shop. There was another shop, but I've forgotten what they sold.

My paper round took me to Elmbridge Road, The Lowe, Manford Way, Manford Green, Regarder Road and New North Road. Quite a long route. One winter morning I got out of bed at the usual time of five o'clock, looked out of the window and saw about two and a half feet of snow on the ground. I went to my parent's bedroom to let them know, as my Dad was due at work. I got my papers delivered and when I got to Huntsman Road I saw a road sweeper outside their small depot, looking at his broom and wondering how he'd work today. I don't know why but I had to do something. I stood about fifteen yards in front, made a big snowball and threw it right at him, catching him on the side of the head and knocking him over. I ran all the way home with him chasing me. I darted indoors and up to my room. There was a knock on the door and my mum answered. The road sweeper told her what happened and my asked how he knew it was her boy. He replied that I was wearing a black coat with sticks on it. This was more commonly known as a duffel coat. I did get a telling off though I later heard my mother telling my dad and they were giggling.

At this time, we never had a television. I remember my Dad going to Bairds and getting one 'on the weekly'. The following week he went to pay and found the shop empty. Someone said the owner had fled to South Africa.

I didn't watch a lot of television, but I did like Billy Bunter, maybe because he was fat and you didn't get many fat boys in Hainault. We had a new neighbour move next door, called Mr Guyaski. He was from Czechoslovakia and had a lovely family, with a young son and daughter. Mr Guyaski had been tortured during the war and had trouble bending over when gardening. He found work at Hainault Station. My other neighbours were Mr Buttery, the Cousins, the Coots, the Cunnighams and Mr Greaves, who had a son called Jimmy, who played football. Further along was Mr Davey, the Meedons and my old mate Johnny Bellyou.

I loved the six-week's holiday away from school. No teachers, no caning and I could do what I wanted. The Fairground always came for ten days, on the field behind our garden. Once, I went over on the day the arrived and got talking to one of the women. She asked if I wanted a job and before you could say 'jack rat' I was working for her. I had to start at nine in the morning and finished late afternoons, for five shillings a day. I had to clean all the boots and shoes, sweep the caravan and man the stall. It was a lucky dip where people picked a straw then pulled out a little ticket to see what prize they could win. It was my job to entice punters to buy the straws. I enjoyed doing that as I could be myself and being an East-ender, had the gift of the gab.

After the fair had left town, we were off to Bognor Regis for a week's holiday in a caravan. We'd heard of Bognor, so it must be good! The journey was nearly a hundred miles and would take about three hours in our Wyvern. When it was time to go the car was packed with suitcases and the four of us children in the back seat. About half an hour into the journey when I first said, "are we there yet?". Nearer to our destination we had to drive up a very steep hill and just about made it.

Our caravan was quite close to the beach and I think my Dad had chosen well as he had no more driving to do. This was his holiday and the rest of us would just get on with it. Most of my Dad's friends had holidays of Hop-picking to fund their food and keep but my father never wanted to work on his holidays. As a family we enjoyed our days on the beach, making the most of it and making new friends. My father was well at home with a pub nearby and we always seemed to have good weather, unlike today where forecasters are getting wrong all the time! It wasn't long before we were homeward bound to Hainault, to carry on with our lives.

In Manford Way one morning I saw a sign in a shop window for an evening paper round. I was now in the money with two rounds and things were looking up. I walked round to a friend's house one morning to see how he was doing. His name was Tommy Stean and it's funny really that he never called me by my first name. It was always 'Martinson' this and 'Martinson' that. I think it might have been because he'd heard the teachers calling my name out all the time.

I got to his house and he said, "what do you want, Martinson?". I asked if he wanted to play outside and he said he'd like to build a go-kart. But first, we had to go over the back field to see if we could find an old pram someone had dumped, for the wheels. We managed to find a couple and before long had the wheels off. Tommy said the next thing we needed was wood to make the kart with and he knew where to get some. There was a wood factory nearby that had a lot off half-cuts at the back of the yard. Tommy said "Martinson, you get over the fence and I'll tell you what we need." I said he should go, but he claimed he couldn't climb it and as it was a Sunday morning there wouldn't be anyone around. So over I went. I threw all the wood we needed back over the fence and we made our way to his house. We were in his back garden when his Dad came out and asked where we'd got all that wood. Tommy replied that 'Martinson' had got it for the go-kart. His Dad said the wood was too good for a kart and he needed it to patch up his shed, so he gave us a bit of scaffold board and some other bits and before long we had our kart. We took it onto the street outside and Tommy said the best place to test it was Hog Hill. I thought it was too steep, but he insisted we go there. So, there we were, at the top of Hog Hill and Tommy said, jump on. I refused but he insisted I drive, so in I jumped. I said he should get on the back, but he took no notice and instead gave it a shove and I was off, going so fast I just knew I was going to crash, either in the road or into a fence. I crashed into a fence, and got up battered and bruised, waiting for Tommy to get to me. A few choice words were said, and he pulled the kart home for repairs. I don't think I ever got on a kart after that.

Back home I was doing quite well with my paper round and decided to buy a bike. I'd had a few old ones but wanted something new. I chose a shop on Chigwell Row near the Maypole Inn. The first bike I bought was a

Raleigh for about twelve pounds, on 'the weekly'. Sadly, the shopkeeper didn't disappear off to South Africa.

There's something about a new bike. You feel good when riding it. There wasn't much traffic in the fifties and the bike was good for my paper rounds and running errands for my mum. Whenever she asked for something from the shops I was always willing to go. It was about this time in my life I rarely saw my parents or sisters as I was always out. I popped home now and again for bread and dripping or a jam sandwich. Word had got around the estate that a lorry carrying sweets had overturned in New North Road, spilling its goods all over the place. I was down there like a shot and the driver was walking around in a daze. A few people were helping themselves, so I thought 'why not?'. I picked out all different types of sweets and managed to fill up three carrier bags I'd stuffed into my pockets. By the time I left everyone was tucking in.

In those days it took the police a good half an hour to get the scene and I never did get told off for getting the sweets. Mind you, I did share them.

The Boy Scouts 'bob-a-job' week was coming up and I thought I'd join. The hut was at the back of a church in Arrowsmith Road. I had about twelve jobs to do, from cleaning motors to a bit of gardening, and people gave me more than a 'bob' (a shilling) but I kept the extra money. Well, I had a bike to run so put it down to administration costs.

A few times my father took me to the stock car racing along Barking Road and I really enjoyed that. The smell of the tyres and petrol fumes. I would soon be eleven years old and joining another school. Like my sisters June and Rita, I'd be going to Kingswood Secondary, but there was a shock in store for me. My last day at Manford Way was one of the happiest days of my life. In my view the teachers were bullies and Mrs Bird was in the wrong job. She should have been a dominatrix, whipping and caning for money. She could have earned thousands and I can see her now in her gold-plated wheelchair! Whenever I see a woman in a wheelchair it reminds me of Mrs Bird.

Now comes the shock. My parents receive a letter informing them I'll be travelling by coach each day to the Warren Secondary School. I'm not wanted in Hainault.

Chapter Three

The Warren Secondary School

Here I am. I've just finished the six-week's holiday and I'm at the coach stop in Huntsman Road. Also waiting for the coach to arrive are Tommy Cunningham and his friend Peter Sugarman. We're going to travel four miles to the Warren school in Whalebone Lane, Dagenham. The schools in Hainault were overflowing so they shipped us out and the coach picks up a couple of girls on route.

The good thing about travelling by coach was that when there was a bad snowfall it never turned up as it couldn't get up Hog Hill. It was so steep they just about made it in good weather! The coaches were always very noisy. They would have been as I was on board! We usually got to school in about twenty minutes, so the journey wasn't that bad.

Mr Davis was the Headmaster and his deputy was Mr Lamb. There was also a Mr Linton-Smith, Mrs Ironmonger, Miss White and Mr Farmer. Out of all the teachers, Mr Lamb was the one to watch. He was very handy with the cane. And as with any school, it had its bullies. The teacher I got along with best was Mr Linton-Smith, who taught art. Miss White did religious instruction and didn't like me. The feeling was mutual. But generally, things were going well for me in the first year and I only got the cane once. I was being bullied by some older boys but took it in my stride. Mr Lamb once saw me looking at his car during a dinner break and asked me if I wanted to clean it. I agreed and every fortnight from then on, I gave it a clean during dinner time and got two and sixpence, and the cane the following day if I was unlucky. Mr Lamb also gave gardening lessons which I enjoyed. However, I didn't enjoy PT (physical training). It was alright if you were inside, in the main hall but not when you had to do five miles cross-country running.

One morning I woke up at 5am and was getting ready for my paper round. Looking out of the window I could see about a foot of snow, and it was still falling. I did my round on foot, went back home for breakfast which was most probably bread and dripping, then went to the coach stop and was told to go home as the coach wouldn't be coming. When I got back home my mother asked me to go to Manford Way shops with her. As we were getting near to the shops, a man came up to us and said, "what have we got here then?". He was from the school board. I replied, "a boy and his mother" and mum told me not to be so cheeky. He asked why I wasn't at school and my mother replied that I went to the Warren and there were no coaches. As he left I flashed him a cheeky grin.

The weather was quite bad for the next few days, so I missed more school. Most of my friends in Hainault had no idea what they would do for work when they left school and I was much the same. I knew I would find work and that when I turned twenty-one I'd get my docker or stevedore ticket. In my second year at the Warren we had a new teacher, Mr Farmer. He looked and talked like a farmer too, and I must admit I was a git towards him in the classroom. I'm sorry to say but if I find a weakness in someone I'll work on it. I suppose it was because I was being bullied at the time, so I took it out on the teachers. I know it was wrong but at the time it couldn't be helped. We were in the classroom one day and Mr Farmer was chalking something on the blackboard when I made a noise like 'Moooo' and quickly put my head down. He demanded to know who did it but when no one answered he went back to the blackboard, looking back over his shoulder occasionally. I then went 'Miaowww'. The blackboard rubber came flying across the classroom aimed at no-one. I calmly asked if everything was alright and Mr Farmer replied that he wanted to know who was responsible for the animal noises. Again, no one owned up and I didn't make any more noises. I'm sorry Mr Farmer. It was me.

Back in Hainault, my sister June had left school and started working in a bank in London. Family life went on with my mother still doing all the painting around the house. Sometimes one of her brothers would visit from Richmond to help. She used to take us children over to Richmond by train to see my grandmother but there were always rows. More about that later.

We still went over to Canning Town on a Saturday afternoon, to Rathbone Market. Sometimes we'd stay over if my aunt Francis has one of her parties. The piano would come out the children would look on in amazement at uncles and aunts gathering round it to sing. You can't beat an East-End party.

By this time, I was starting to appreciate girls but was very shy in that department, though there were plenty of pretty girls in Hainault. One day I went to Tommy's house and he wanted to go to Hainault Forest. So off we go on a nice sunny afternoon and get talking to two girls, one more pretty than the other. Tommy asked the one who wasn't so pretty if she wanted to go into the bushes with him and she agreed. I was left with the pretty one and made some small talk. It wasn't long before Tommy and his new friend re-emerged, and the girls went home. On our way home, a man stopped us and said he'd give us two shillings and sixpence if we played with his willy. Tommy said, "Martinson will". I said, "Martinson won't!" and we both ran home. Thanks for that Tommy! I was too scared to tell my parents as I'd never been in that kind of situation before. If I'd told my Dad, he would have hunted him down.

Back at the Warren during my last year I had the cane about four times. Not too bad I suppose. I'd started skipping lunch break and spending my shilling in Anne's store over the road from the school. I'd get a Mars Bar and a Jubbly drink and still have change. I'd then walk up to Chadwell Heath High Road to get some chips. My good friends then were Peter Dawson and Kenneth Beagle. The last time I saw Peter was in Falmouth when he was about to sail on a Blue Funnel Ship, to where I don't know. Kenneth was shot dead in 2000 outside Oldchurch Hospital in what was thought to be a drug deal gone wrong. He was 55 years old.

One thing I didn't agree with was the compulsory boxing matches. To me it was often a mismatch for any pupil the teachers didn't like. I'm sure they put you in the ring with someone who would knock you about. I was once put in the ring with a bully and feigned injury to get my fight over. I also remember harvest festival at the Warren when every pupil brought something in. It was quite a sight to see all the fruit and vegetables lined up on the stage and I don't know whether it went to the pensioners or the teachers. Mr Linton-Smith was our art teacher and the best teacher I knew. He really could get the best out of you and gave you time. A good friend of mine, Harry Meacher, who is now an actor, director and playwright; and is married to Judi Bowker of Black Beauty fame, really got on well with Mr Linton-Smith and I wouldn't be surprised if he'd helped him to get where he is now. Harry put on a play at the end of the year before we left for good. It was Scrooge and we all helped paint the background scenes. Though I couldn't get out of my mind that although I was his best mate he put me in the role of a beggar. Well, I know I'm a cockney, but a beggar? Oh well. The play went down really well and I'm glad for Harry. I was always with him in the late fifties, especially going to the cinema to see films like Joan of Arc or the Lion in Winter. He couldn't get enough of them. I'd love to still be in touch with Harry.

It was near to the last day of school that I had my assessment interview. It didn't go well, and I was told the nearest thing I'd got for work was sweeping up in the factories on the Hainault Industrial Estate. One week later I was back in front of the assessors telling them I was starting work in the London Stock Exchange. I gave them a grin as if to say, 'up yours'. He was shocked, and to be honest so was I. So how did I do it?

Chapter Four

Working in London

I've left school and need to go to Barkingside to get myself a suit, some shirts and new shoes as I can't go to work looking like a scruff. Although I'd told the teacher I was going to work at the Stock Exchange, it was the foreign exchange, but the former sounded more glamorous. So, in 1959 I started working for Savage and Heath in Frogmorton Street next to the Bank of England and opposite the Stock Exchange. You couldn't get more central to the heart of Britain.

My job in the company was that of messenger and typist. They paid for me to go to typing classes one evening each week and after a couple of weeks I was typing out invoices and taking them round to the banks. I must have visited every bank in London and loved chatting to all the girls on reception. I can't remember fully but think I was getting about four pounds fifty pence a week and a bonus of one percent commission. My season ticket was twelve and six shillings per week.

I'd been working there for around six months when I met my first girlfriend, who we'll call Gloria. She was a pretty girl from Hainault and we'd see each other a couple of times in the week and at weekends, when we'd go shopping or visiting friends and family. At work I was constantly being asked to make the tea and coffee for visiting clients. The office didn't employ women so there was only me and two other men and the boardroom, where there were eight men who sat trading currency. We knew when a good trade had been made as there would be shouts from the boardroom, so a good commission was coming our way. I always got at least ten pounds commission each month.

I stayed with Savage and Heath for about a year and a half, but I was getting nowhere. I was still young and wanted some excitement. One of my Dads brothers, Tommy, worked as a Foreman for the New Zealand Shipping Company in the Royal Albert Docks and put a word in for me to see if the company would let me join the Merchant Navy. I was accepted and handed in my notice at Savage and Heath. A new life was about to begin.

Chapter Five

Romford Police Station

A little side story. I was with a couple of my friends, Frank Coot and John Bellyou, both good friends from Huntsman Road, and we were walking the streets with our transistor radio blaring out. Around seven o'clock that evening we decided to go to Romford on the bus. We all had our suits on and I was wearing a green Robin Hood style hat with a feather sticking out the side.

When we were on the bus Frank said he had something to show us and took out a gun from his pocket. I said I'd had one of those when I played cowboys and Indians years ago, but Frank insisted it was the real thing and asked us to feel the weight of it. It was very heavy and real. So, I waved it around a bit before Frank took it back and put it away. When we got off the bus and were walking down to Market Street a policeman approached us and said "alright, who's got the gun?". Frank pulled it from his pocket and asked if that was what he was looking for. The policeman took a step back then pounced on him. We were all taken to Romford Station and put in separate rooms. After a while, a detective came in and asked who I was. He then asked why I was wearing that stupid hat and I could only reply that it was the fashion. He asked me a few questions about the gun and said he was sure my picture was on his mug sheets. In fact, he thought I was dodgy looking and was sure he'd seen me in a suspect picture a few weeks ago, from a robbery at a local factory.

He then left, and I thought I was going to be stitched up for someone else's crime, but about half an hour later he returned and said I was free to go. I got outside, and John was waiting for me to get the bus home. Later, Frank's mum and dad had to go with him to Romford Station where he was given a caution. It turns out he'd borrowed it from a cupboard where he worked to show it to us. It's something we laugh about now though we didn't at the time!

Chapter Six

In the Navy Now

It was a Monday when I arrived at the gates of the Merchant Navy College in Gravesend, Kent. They were going to whip me into shape, so I could start work as a steward on board one of their ships. I was one of about fifteen boys and we all got on well together. Our first lesson was how to make our bunk beds. If the bed wasn't made properly the Chief Steward would pull the blankets off and we'd have to make it again. We did this, day in, day out for six weeks along with other lessons including how to lay a table with full silver service.

During the six weeks of training, three boys left. I guess they missed their mums. We were allowed out of our dormitory on a couple of nights but had to be in full uniform including a beret which made us a target for local boys. Picture the scene, a group of young Frank Spencer lookalikes walking around! We were also allowed home once during this time and those who did got themselves a railway warrant. All in all, I enjoyed my time at the college. We had a lot of pep talks and before long it was time to go out and find ourselves a ship.

The ship I joined was the MV Rangitani, a passenger ship that took emigrants to Australia under the assisted passenger scheme, or the 'Ten Pound Poms' as they were known. People got full board and lodging for their journey and at the end reached their promised land. I joined the ship on a Thursday morning and was taken to the Chief Stewards cabin. His first words to me were "why are you wearing that stupid uniform?" I replied that I thought we had to wear it, but he told me I should have ditched it as soon as I got out of college. He then took me to my cabin to meet the person I'd share it with. The door was opened, and a man greeted me. The Chief Steward introduced me to 'Daisy' who he said would show me the ropes, and then off he went.

I hadn't been in the cabin long and had to ask why he was called Daisy but was just told that was the name he was known by. I was still confused when he took me to meet his mates so off we went along the corridor and knocked at another cabin. Daisy then introduced me to Mollie who beckoned us inside and I saw another man sitting on the bunk bed, who was introduced to me as Sadie. By now I was really confused, wondering what I'd walked into and what was I doing here? The cabin stank of perfume and I was beginning to get high on the fumes. I said I should go and get unpacked so left quickly.

Later, I was in the mess room and got talking to a couple of men who informed me that my new roommate and his friends were gay and if I told them I wasn't interested then they'd leave me alone. Back in the cabin I was still unpacking when Daisy came in and pointed to the bunk that was mine for the trip. I'd noticed an engraving on the back of my locker door that read 'Tommy Hicks' and asked Daisy if she knew who it was. She told me it was an old cabin mate who'd entertained the crew with his guitar playing. So, I was now going to be sleeping in Tommy Steele's bunk bed! Daisy asked if I'd any Wrangler jeans as men would come on board when we got to Australia and buy them at a really good price. The following morning, I went out and bought six pairs. We set sail on the Saturday morning, travelling first to Tilbury to pick up the passengers.

When we arrived in Tilbury and the passengers started boarding you could tell that some were more excited than others about the journey. Most of them gave us tips which I liked, and then at one o'clock in the afternoon it was anchor up and away we went, with those on-board waving goodbyes to friends and family, not knowing if they'd ever see them again. Our first destination was Curacao, a tropical island in the Caribbean and part of the Dutch West Indies. There was a running buffet that afternoon as most of the passengers were still unpacking. Daisy warned me not to expect tips from the passengers at the end of our journey as they were not fare paying and needed all the money they had. There were two sittings for dinner in the evening and on the first day everything went well for me. I had five tables to look after and always the same passengers to serve. It was hard work but enjoyable, carrying four plates at once through a crowded dining-room was quite daunting, especially in rough seas.

A few days into the trip I noticed some of the passengers were missing from my tables and was told it was due to sea-sickness. Luckily, I didn't suffer from it and quite enjoyed a bit of rough weather. When all the passengers had finished their meals, it was a bit of a rush to get everything ready for breakfast the following morning. After I'd finished my first shift I was able to get to know my fellow crew members a bit better and they became a nice bunch of mates. That evening I met Sadie and Mollie in the corridor, coming towards me in full drag. I was wondering if I could deal with this and when I got to my cabin I asked Daisy if he also liked to dress up in women's clothes. He said he didn't which was a bit of a relief and I was further reassured after telling him I was totally straight, though I did like him as a person!

There was a shop on board where you could buy cigarettes and sweets amongst other things, but I couldn't buy beer as I was still under-age. It was a British registered ship with British laws. When you bought cigarettes, you didn't pay in cash as it was deducted from our pay at the end of the trip.

We eventually docked in Curacao and the passengers disembarked to stretch their legs for a while. Some of the crew members wanted to go to a place called 'Happy Valley' which was a large building in the middle of the desert that housed 'good-time' girls. I took the opportunity to have a drink while I was there but didn't join in when some of the others went off to the rooms. I was starting to see a bit of life!

Before long we were on our way to Panama. The Panama Canal is an artificial, forty-eight-mile waterway that connects the Atlantic and Pacific Oceans. We were awaiting our turn to enter the locks and eventually the ship was pulled through by Mule 'trains'. This took around eight hours and we were then on our way to Tahiti, a place I'd read about and couldn't wait to see. Life on board carried on and I was happy. Serving breakfast wasn't quite as hectic as evening mealtimes but was still a rush to serve the twelve-people seated on my tables, all the while knowing I wouldn't get any tips at the end. We docked in Papeete and I was excited to join my friends at the Bamboo Hut where you could buy beer and chat up the local girls. I couldn't wait until the passengers were off the ship, on their excursions. I was told the Tahitians took ages to do everything, so I got four beers instead of two, otherwise I'd have been queuing up for a long time. We were inside the Bamboo Hut and I had my four beers. A pretty girl smiled at me and I asked if she wanted to join me for a drink on the beach. She agreed and smiled again, which was when I noticed she didn't have the best teeth. Apparently, a lot of Tahitians didn't have great teeth at that time due to the water. But still, off we went to the beach and I was sitting there with a pretty, native girl (when she had her mouth shut). I wondered to myself what the teachers at the Warren School would think if they could see me now.

Soon it was time to get back the ship and my duties on board. So, I kissed my native girl goodbye (again, mouth closed) and promised I'd meet her when the ship returned. Her name was Tia.

The passengers were returning and seemed happy, on the final leg of their journey to the promised land. I wondered what was going through their minds. Would they like Australia or eventually return home? Although the trip took six weeks for passengers, for the crew it was more like four months because of all the loading and unloading of cargo. On the outward voyage we'd take cars, tractors and all other sorts of cargo and going back to England it would be mostly frozen lamb!

We had fun on board in the evenings, playing table-tennis, cards or just drinking. Someone would slip me a crafty beer now and again. Mollie and Sadie sometimes put on a show and it was all good, clean fun. Once a week, Captain Rees would carry out an inspection where he would look in all the cabins and galleys.

On the last day at sea, many of the passengers looked forlorn. I guess they were wondering what awaited them when they left the ship. They'd been on board for nearly one hundred days, on the longest holiday of their lives not having to pay for anything except their drinks. We arrived in Sydney and I was serving the final meal. It was sad as they'd come to feel like family and shook my hand and thanked me for my service. I did get a tip from a few of them and was grateful.

Once the passengers had left it was like a ghost ship. On my days off I managed to get a ticket to work dockside, loading up on the quay. The men wanting to buy jeans came aboard and bartered with me. When we'd agreed a price, I was given a list of what to bring on the next trip. Our time in Sydney was made up of going into town, wandering round the shops and visiting a café called 'The Coffin', where they had coffin lids as tables! I was also legally allowed to drink beer.

We left for Auckland in New Zealand to load up with more lamb and pick up our fare-paying passengers for the journey to England. I didn't like New Zealand as much as Australia, but I did like the sausage and chip vans on every street corner in Auckland.

I was now greeting the passengers at my five tables for dinner, treating them with a lot of respect as there was a good chance of tips at the end of this journey. We sailed to Pitcairn Island which is one of a group of four volcanic islands in the Southern Pacific and had a population of about sixty. We moored nearby as our ship was too big for the port. Then we were off again to Tahiti. It was very hot at night and some of us slept in the hatches. I remember taking salt-tablets as well when we were in the tropics. Tia was nowhere to be found so I went to Quinns, a notorious bar and had a drink with my mates. We didn't stay long as if we'd been late back it'd be a strike against our name.

The ship had its own newspaper which consisted of a couple of sheets, outlining what was going on around the world. The only time any of us saw Captain Rees was on his weekly inspection. He was God on board and the ship was his kingdom. He even had guns in his locker, in case he thought his life was ever in danger. We passed through the Panama Canal and docked in Curacao and finally arrived back in Tilbury.

From there we sailed to the Royal Group of Docks to discharge our cargo. When we arrived, the customs officers came on board to check our cabins and make sure we only had the permitted amount of duty. We signed-off from the trip and had the choice of re-signing to another voyage if we wanted to. I did so and was told to re-join the ship in ten days' time. It was custom to give the policeman on the dock gate ten shillings, so we'd be quickly on our way instead of having our suitcases checked. Before long I was back in Hainault and glad to see my parents and sisters, as well as my girlfriend. I'd bought them all gifts and whilst I was away had sixteen pounds sent back to my mother every month. This was for my board and keep even though I wasn't living there.

In no time I was re-joining the Rangitani with the same crew and was sharing with Daisy again. This was a similar journey and I was keen to get a different ship and route next time. When I got to Australia I met the 'jeans man' and had all the things he'd asked for. Lots of lovely money for me! About this time, the Beatles had arrived in Australia and people were going crazy for them. There was nothing but the Beatles on the radio and television and I got a bit fed up with it in the end. When we set sail on our homeward voyage I was told that Captain Rees wanted to see me. I thought it strange as no one ever seemed to go to his quarters except the officers.

I'll always remember the day, 19th December 1964. I knocked on his door and he told me to enter. As soon as I was inside he said, "Your Mum's dead". I could only ask "what?" and he repeated himself. Naturally, I started crying and he asked why. I said that it was because it was Christmas and he replied that every day was Christmas. He gave me a bottle of whisky and told me I was relieved of duties for the rest of the day, and to resume work in the morning. The rest of the voyage was a blur and I could not wait to get back home. A lot of things crossed my mind during that journey, wondering how my little sister had taken the news, who had been at the funeral and how my dad was coping. I also wondered if they'd be thinking of me.

Once the trip ended I was signing-off and seeking a new route. Back home in Hainault there was a tearful reunion. It was hard to accept what had happened. My mother had died of a brain haemorrhage and had spent her last week in hospital.

My sister Linda took over the cooking as my dad couldn't boil an egg. He gave her money for shopping and still didn't lift a finger at home. My girlfriend seemed a bit distant as well and it began to play on my mind. I was at home for about a week but in all honesty, I wanted to get back to sea. The following day I went to the Pool of London, the office where they informed you what ships required crew. The man there asked if I wanted to join the Loch Gowan which was sailing to Bermuda, Trinidad and Columbia as the Royal Mail Line, taking mail and cargo. That would do me!

The ship was also due to visit ports along the west coast of America, then Vancouver before returning home. I was told to come back the next morning and I'd be taken to Gatwick Airport where I'd get a plane to Hamburg in Germany, to pick up the ship when it docked for repairs. I was worried as I didn't have a passport but was informed that my discharge book was my passport. I rushed home and packed up, saying my goodbyes to everyone.

I'd never been on a plane before and was really excited about this new experience. There were eight of us on the transport to the airport and we soon got to know each other. I enjoyed the flight and before long we were in Hamburg. We caught a coach to the ship and once I was on board I was told my job was Mess Man. Basically, I oversaw the mess room where the crew were fed. I soon made friends and that evening went ashore with a couple of them to see what was around. There were shops and clubs everywhere and we ended up in a place called 'Bordelstrasse' where women paraded around in skimpy outfits, plying their trade. That was another eye-opener!

I wondered what Mrs Bird from Manford Way would think if she could have seen me then. We enjoyed looking at the women but that was as far as the fun went. We got back to the ship and sailed the following day. Just as we sailed out we ran into another ship and sank it. Fortunately, all lives were saved, and we limped back into port, where we stayed for about ten days for further repairs.

We couldn't go out as we were all skint so stuck to a few beers every now and then. I got along well with the crew who were a lovely bunch. There were no Mollie's or Sadie's about either. Eventually we upped anchor and were on our way to Bermuda for a short stop before onwards to Trinidad. When we docked we saw young boys diving into the water on the dockside for money the crew were throwing in. The water was crystal clear, a wonderful sight.

We went to a few bars for a drink but were only in port for twelve hours before setting sail for New York. On board it was just working, reading and wandering around on deck, thinking about how life was going on with my family. My sister June was courting a young man called Bob and I was looking forward to reaching New York to see if we'd had any more mail and there was any more news. I did have a letter, but it was from my girlfriend Gloria and was a 'Dear John'. This is the type of mail all seamen hate to receive as you're so far from home, and it did hurt, but life went on.

We were in New York for a couple of nights and a few of us thought we'd go to the cinema, which started at ten o'clock at night and finished at five in the morning. It was showing three Audie Murphy films for a dollar. At about midnight we looked around and everyone was sleeping in their seats. It was a glorified doss-house! And later that night to add to the excitement, the manager started chasing a guy around, waving a gun!

But I loved New York and vowed to return. Our next stop was Los Angeles, but we were only there for a day, so I didn't get to go ashore, but looking forward to reaching San Francisco. I had a great time there, seeking out the hippies, and we found quite a few. One evening I sat on the shore looking at Alcatraz and wondering how the prisoners were feeling. I could see the lights from the prison going back and forth. I'd read about the place and seen films set there, such as the Birdman of Alcatraz with Burt Lancaster as the leading man. The shops and coffee houses there were better than back home but to get into the clubs and bars you needed to show identification as you had to be over twenty-one.

Our next port of call was Fort Lauderdale. We berthed in the afternoon and by the early evening were wondering what to do when two men came aboard and said to me "Do you want to go to a party...?"

Chapter Seven

Partying in the Hollywood Mansions

I called over to my friends to ask if they wanted to join me at a party in Hollywood and they naturally agreed. I asked one of the men what we should wear, and he suggested jeans and a shirt. They said they would pick us up at eight and come the time a Limousine drew up with the same two men inside. We got in and drove away, watching our fellow crew members look on in astonishment.

It wasn't long before we arrived at a huge mansion in the Hollywood hills. I remember seeing a lot of expensive cars outside the mansion and wonder who they belonged to. We went inside and shook hands with a few people. Some of the women looked like movie stars and there were a few Mollie's and Sadie's around! I warned my friends to stick to the bottled beer as the drinks could be spiked. It had crossed my mind that there might be a more sinister reason for the invitation, but I genuinely think they just wanted a few people from England to mix with. There was plenty of music and dancing and we were groped a few times but only in a jokey way. The party was really swinging, and we were having a great time, eventually returning to our ship at two in the morning.

We sailed on the next day to Galveston, Texas and then to Vancouver and finally back to London. When I got back I thought I'd try for a different route and got a job on board the Northern Star, a cruise ship that went to Durban, Cape Town, Sydney and a few other places. I was back as a waiter, meaning tips from passengers which I loved. I don't recall much about that trip, but my final voyage was on board what was then the biggest tanker in the world, sailing from the Isle of Grain in Kent to Tripoli and back. I was Mess Man on that ship and remember than when we reached Tripoli all you could see was sand and desert for miles and miles. When I got back from that trip I thought it was time to stay on dry land.

Chapter Eight

Back Home

I'm back in Hainault and I've got to get a job. I've done the rounds and visited all my friends. Some are courting and others still single. My sister Rita is courting a man called Dennis Dell who was soon to become the lead singer in the Honeycombs. They had a hit song with 'Have I the Right?' which shot to the top of the hit parade. They were also rare in their time for having a female drummer.

I managed to get a job at a suitcase factory called Cla Rev, in Roebuck Road. I began using the Old Maypole as my local pub, in Fencepiece Road, Barkingside. It was a nice, friendly pub run by Doug and his wife Lynn. After a couple of months at the suitcase factory I saw an advert for London Transport so sent off my application.

Whilst waiting for a reply, me and a few friends decided to go to London one Saturday. One of my pals didn't have any money for a ticket so I said I'd get one for him. Back at home I found my old season ticket to Liverpool Street and quickly altered the dates. I was quite proud of the job I'd done. On the day I gave my friend the ticket and bought my own. We caught the train to Liverpool Street and when we got off, showed our tickets to the attendant. My friend was stopped, and the Transport Police were called. We both got prosecuted for having a forged ticket; him for travelling with it and me for doing the forging!

In the meantime, working at Cla Rev wasn't for me. I didn't enjoy working from bell to bell. One evening when I got home there were two letters waiting for me to open. One told me I was due in court on Tuesday and the other from London Transport, inviting me for an interview! At court I was fined £10 and the magistrate grinned when he said I'd never become a master forger. Later that week I was offered a job on the Permanent Way, on the night shift. I would be based at the depot at Marble Arch, on the Central Line. One of the first things I had to do was collect my train pass. A genuine one this time!

I handed in my notice at Cla Rev and soon started working on the London Underground. It was a good job, repairing damaged tracks and renewing sleepers. We had to wait for the electricity to be turned off before we could enter the track and had our own lighting for the tunnels. It was hard work, but the pay was good. We started just after midnight and always finished by quarter past five the next morning.

Around this time, I bought my first car, a Hillman Imp. I was driving around with L Plates, but it did have insurance. I visited my friend Tommy's house to show him my pride and joy. Tommy had also bought a car, but I can't remember the model. When it came time to leave my car wouldn't start so Tommy's dad said he'd give me a tow. He owned a van with two small bumpers at the rear to which he tied a rope and then attached it to my car. He told me that when he put his hand out of the window I should put my car into second gear and let the clutch out slowly. Tommy and I got into my car and when we got up to a certain speed Tommy's dad put his hand out as planned, but instead of putting my car into second as I'd been told, I put my foot on the brake, resulting in both his small rear bumpers flying over the top of my car. Tommy and I both started laughing but were out of the car and running as fast as we could with his dad in pursuit! I thought he'd kill me but when I returned and offered to pay for the damage everything was fine. It turned out all my car had needed was a new battery.

My sister June married Bob and they moved away to a flat near Cranbrook Road in Ilford. I was still at home and getting into more arguments with my father who wasn't pulling his weight as far as I was concerned. Most of it fell to Rita and Linda as I was on the Underground and enjoying the freedom.

Chapter Nine

At the Old Bailey

Now I had a legitimate railway pass I used it to go and meet my cousin George and his mates in Stratford. His pals were Paul Williamson, Billy Barlow, George Brand and another called Danny, but I can't recall his surname. We went for a few drinks and started at the Black Bull which was usually full of jolly Irishmen. We then moved on a few steps to the Two Puddings where they had a long saloon bar on the ground level and dancing area upstairs. The place was run by Eddie and Kenny Johnson and I met some wonderful friends there, as well as my future wife.

My local in Hainault at the time was the Old Maypole which I visited a couple of times during the week. I also went to another pub called the Alfred's Head in Manford Way every now and again, as it was usually where I could find my Dad. One evening I met a friend, Terry Pritchard, for a drink and we headed to the Old Maypole. It was a Friday night and the place was crowded, with the juke box blaring out the latest tunes. Terry was talking to a man at the bar who didn't look pleased and suddenly pushed a glass into Terry's face, cutting him badly. Doug, the publican, gave him a towel to stem the blood and called an ambulance which arrived quickly and took Terry off to King George Hospital in Redbridge. I went with him to help in any way I could.

The man who'd glassed him had fled the scene and when Terry was stitched up we went to Barkingside Police Station to make our statements. It transpired that Terry knew the man, but they didn't like each other. The man lived on the prefab estate near Elmbridge Road, close to my house. Before long we were at the Old Bailey, giving evidence. I entered the Witness Box and the lawyer for the defence asked if I was a good friend of Terry. I said I was and he asked if I'd do anything for him, to which I replied I would, but only lawfully. He didn't have any further questions. The man was later found guilty of Grievous Bodily Harm and sentenced to four and a half years in prison. The whole experience, including walking into that building gave me shivers.

I was still working on the railways but counting the days until I could go back into the docks. I was also thinking of leaving home at this point due to the constant rows with my dad. Despite our differences he put in a notice that I wanted to join the Dockworkers Union and within a couple of weeks it was done and dusted and just after turning twenty-one years old I was accepted as a dockworker. I had plenty to celebrate and took my dad out for a drink that evening. I said my goodbyes to my friends on the Underground, but the hardest thing was giving up my free rail pass!

Chapter Ten

A Stevedore and a Docker

Working in the docks was something I'd looked forward to doing. My first day was on the Stones, where dockers stood and gang masters picked the men they wanted to work for them. It was tough as some men weren't picked but got a credit and a bit of money for turning up. I was lucky that morning as a ganger waved me through. I met the other gang members and told them it was my first day. The ganger informed me he was told to pick me by my Uncle Tom, who worked for the New Zealand Shipping Company.

My first ship to unload was the Rangitani, the one I'd sailed away to Australia on a few years ago. We started unloading the general cargo and deeper down in the holds was the frozen lamb.

Most of the dockers had nicknames and I was trying to remember them all, as they all had a reason behind them. We had a break halfway through our shift and a mobile canteen would draw up. I queued up for something to eat and when I got to the counter I was given a cup of tea and saw they had slices of bread and dripping for sale at two-pence each. I asked for three crusts and was in heaven. I'd not had bread and dripping since my mum passed away.

The next day I didn't need to go on the Stones as we had to see our work on the ship through to the day it sailed. I had to work a week in hand so didn't get paid straight away for unloading all that frozen lamb. It was hard graft, but I was getting used to it and making a new set of friends. When we were near to finishing loading the ship, the ganger asked if I wanted to stay in his gang and I agreed, meaning I wouldn't need to go on the Stones again.

We finally finished loading the Rangitani and as I was about to leave I looked behind me and saw, standing there with their suitcases, ready for the voyage, were Daisy, Mollie and Sadie. They were really pleased I'd found a job in the docks and we bid each other a fond farewell. I also saw some other crew members I recognised, including Captain Rees who I made a point of speaking to, asking if he remembered me. He replied that he did and wished me good luck before going up the gangplank.

When I got my first pay packet it was more than double what I'd been earning at London Underground and was told it was because we were doing piecework, and the more lamb you unloaded, the more money you got.

Back at home my father was dating a woman from Stratford and my sister Rita was courting a young man called Ray. My other sister, Linda, was keeping the house going as well as doing her job in a Chocolate Factory on the Hainault Industrial Estate.

I decided to enjoy my money and went off to Granitors, a Menswear Shop in Canning Town where I requested a made-to-measure suit. I picked out the colour and style and was told to come back in a week for the fitting. The colour I chose was then known, genuinely, as 'nigger brown'. Not a colour you can get these days!

Back in the docks I was told to get a pair of boots, some overalls and gloves from the storeroom. These were issued annually, and my next job was on an Indian ship that carried a cargo of tea. You could smell the aroma from these ships coming up the Thames!

Most gangs had a man who would make the tea during the breaks to save us going to the canteen although I always went there for my bread and dripping. I was told by my mates that the next pay packet wouldn't be as good due to the cargo we were unloading. When we started moving the crates into the shed, our tea man knew the crates to open and mixed up the different tea-leaves into a large bag that lasted us for months.

I remember working on a Banana Boat in the Tidal Basin. There were always green bananas left on the quayside that were going to the rubbish cart and we could take them home. I couldn't understand it, as you only needed to wait a few days and they would be ripe.

A week passed, and I went to have my suit fitting. I was then to collect it the following week. I'd worked on a few ships now and was still meeting my cousin and his friends for a drink or two in the Two Puddings. I was complimented on my suit when I finally got it and wore it out one evening. About this time, I bought my next vehicle, a van, despite not yet passing my test. A friend helped me to pass it soon afterwards.

Christmas at home was always a sad time for me since mum passed away and I tried to stay out as much as possible. I went to a few parties around the East End and couldn't wait to get back to work. I was twenty-two now and took a few girls out but none of them were going to be my true love. I continued to earn well in the docks and had a good group of friends. I made sure I got my bread and dripping every day and had a couple of pints in the public house in the docks. The work was tiring, dirty and sometimes dangerous. There were a lot of unpleasant materials we had to deal with such as iodine, asbestos, lead and cement, which could all lead to illnesses, and the accident rate was very high.

In my time in the docks I had four accidents. The first was at the Royal Albert Docks when part of the bank gave way when I was throwing frozen lamb into a lorry. It was down to the Port of London Authority (PLA) to make sure the banks were in good condition, but I fell where it gave way and had severe bruising on my back and legs which needed hospital treatment. You did at least get sick pay when you were recovering and could visit a Claims Assessor to see if you had grounds for a claim. Our nearest assessor was a Mr Heenan who had an office in East Ham. If he thought you had a good chance for a claim he'd tell you not to go to work and a few weeks later you received a letter from a specialist in Harley Street, inviting to you to attend so he could assess your injuries.

When I read the report of mine I wondered how I was able to walk. Talk about exaggerated! You usually had to wait around nine months for a payout.

My second happened when I was coming down a metal ladder in the hold. I reached the bottom and when I put my foot down it went right onto a piece of wood with a large nail sticking out of it, going right through my foot. I was off to hospital again, for a tetanus injection and was also given crutches. I was off work for three weeks and on my first day back I put the crutches in the car to take back to the hospital. That day we were loading iron pipes and myself and another man were carrying a pipe when he dropped his end. I had to let go because of the extra weight and it fell on my foot. So, it was another trip to hospital and I'd be off for another month. Whilst I was there, a nurse told me to wait while she got me some crutches and I told her not to bother as I already had some in the car!

My last accident was in the Victoria Docks, working on a barge with a fellow docker called Lionel Clark. The barge was half open, meaning the other half was boarded up and secured by a steel crossbeam. After putting some cargo into the barge, the crane hook raised up and caught the crossbeam, resulting in it falling into the barge with all the boards, on top of me and Lionel. We both had head injuries which were not too bad, but we had to go to hospital and all work on the barge was stopped straight away for the Board of Trade to investigate. Any head injury, no matter how minor, meant you couldn't work for two days afterwards. We both had two weeks off.

About nine months later I bought a copy of the Evening Standard at the dock gate and it said the PLA had been fined fifty thousand pounds for accidents in the docks. So, myself and Lionel were front-page news and we knew our claim would go through. The Royal Group of Docks was to close a few years later and I wonder what happened to Mr Heenan. He must have been a rich man with all that commission and probably has a villa on the Costa Brava.

Chapter Eleven

The Two Puddings and the Docks

I left my gang after about fifteen months as we weren't getting good ships and flitted around other gangs. My father worked on the American ships and I once got placed in his gang to unload for the American air bases around the UK. They used to send across lots of sweets and occasionally we'd open a crate and have a feast. Unfortunately, there was never any drink.

My local was the Two Puddings on Stratford Broadway which I'd frequent most weekends. This was around the time of the World Cup in 1966. When England won I knew the East End would be rocking and couldn't wait to get to the Puddings. Like many East-enders I thought West Ham won the World Cup!

I got off the train around seven in the evening and outside the station people were singing, shouting and drinking along the streets. I knew I was in for a good night. The Puddings was crammed full and everyone was on a high. After closing time, we went to my cousins for a party and it seemed to last forever. There were plenty of Party Sevens, a large can of drink with seven pints in it. I don't think I slept at all that night and ended up back in Hainault around eleven the next morning.

One Tuesday I received a letter informing me I had to go to Moorfields Eye Hospital the following week. I had a small operation and was off work for the next week but there was a strike going on at the time and my father was unhappy as there wasn't any money coming in. On the Saturday evening I bought a newspaper and the headline read 'Man Shot in Soho'. The story was that a nightclub doorman had been shot by a customer and it turned out that the victim was my cousin Roy Martinson. He was the son of my Uncle Tom, who'd got me into the Merchant Navy. I gave the paper to my dad who'd been sleeping off a few earlier pints and he got on the phone to all the family. The gunman was eventually caught and sent to prison.

Following my operation, I had to wear an eye patch for a while and one night I heard screaming so went outside to investigate and saw a neighbour's house on fire. Before the Fire Brigade arrived, I went inside and tried to put it out, but it was too fierce. I was featured in the story in the following week's Ilford Recorder and the photo didn't look too bad considering the eyewear!

After the dock strike had ended I returned to work and picked up a few wage packets but they only had tax rebates in them. I asked the pay clerk why I didn't have any sick pay and he replied that I'd been on strike so wasn't entitled. I sought out Jack Dash, the unofficial Docker's leader and told him what had happened. After all, I'd told my employer I was going into hospital before the strike started. He backed me up and went to the office where they soon agreed to pay me as they didn't want another strike on their hands.

A few days later I joined another gang led by Billy Templeman and we worked mainly at Z Shed on the Argentine ships which mainly carried a cargo of beef. I had to wear a leather scarf on my shoulders and four men would lift a quarter of beef up and place it on my shoulders while I bent over. I'd then run with the heavy load on my shoulders to a lorry and toss it onto the other beef inside. This was one of the top gangs in the docks mainly because of the hard work involved.

Back at the Two Puddings I met a girl who'd come down from Wales for the weekend and knew some of my group of friends. I asked if she wanted to go to a club and she agreed so we went to a new club behind Ilford Railway Station. We had an enjoyable evening and I got her back safely to her friend's house. She invited me to visit her at her parent's house in Neath, near Cardiff. I travelled there and was welcomed with open arms, perhaps because I was in the Transport and General Workers Union and her father was an executive in the Miners Union. I visited Neath a few more times but it fizzled out soon after, although she was a lovely girl.

Although growing up I was a typical mod I would listen to anything that I liked the sound of, such as the Rolling Stones, the Beatles, Bob Dylan, The Shadows, Del Shannon and Roy Orbison. I enjoyed watching Top of the Pops and think the sixties were the best years of my life, what with the miniskirts and sack dresses the girls wore. I remember once asking my sister Rita to dye my hair blonde and she bought some peroxide and did it for me, but it turned out a different colour which I had to live with for months.

Back in Hainault my sister was still acting as housemaid and working at the Chocolate Factory. I had sore shoulders a lot at this time due to my backing beef in the docks. Occasionally we'd get other ships to work but in general I was loving it. My wages had gone up and I was able to get three suits made each year. I loved to look smart and always shopping for shirts and ties. I once bought a suit at Lew Rose, a tailor from Gants Hill near Ilford.

I'd also visit another pub called the Tidal Basin Tavern. It had seen better days, but we had a good arrangement going with the cook. We'd slip him a quarter of beef and he'd make up our beef sandwiches with their homemade bread that melted in your mouth. They went down well with a couple of pints! I also got him to give me pots of beef dripping as I wasn't getting any from home.

Our target was to load three thousand carcasses each day which was back-breaking work. The Clerks on the lorries also had a good arrangement going. Occasionally a quarter of beef would find its way on another lorry and pound notes were given in exchange. When we worked on lamb in another part of the docks a dog would wander in and we'd give it a leg of lamb. It'd then run out past the policeman on the gate with the leg in its mouth. I expect it didn't give the lamb to its owner!

On the way to the docks some of the men would visit cafés for a cup of tea but I went to a house on a back street where the old dear made us tea and toast for a few pence. They had a cardboard sign outside that advertised their teas, but we usually had to make our own toast by holding it in front of a roaring fire. There were a lot of poor families in Canning Town, but they did what they could to get by and were salt of the earth. Sometimes, usually on a Thursday, you'd see women at the dock gates waiting for their husbands, so they could get their housekeeping money before the men could drink or gamble it away.

Chapter Twelve

Family Life

One night in the Two Puddings I spotted two young women standing near to our group and smiled at one of them, who returned it. I asked if they wanted a drink and started chatting to the one who'd smiled back at me. Her name was Pauline and she came from Forest Gate which was just up the road from the pub. We arranged to go for a drink during the week and soon became an item.

Pauline visited our house in Hainault a few times and liked the area. I also went to visit her parents at their flat in Stork Road, which they'd lived in for twenty years. This was in a converted house and theirs was on the upper floor. The flat itself was quite small and had a toilet in the back garden. I felt fortunate to have been living somewhere so spacious and open by comparison.

Back at the docks I'd put in for a St Johns Ambulance course and if I passed, would get another fifteen shillings a week. I managed to pass and was now qualified to help injured dockers as far as my first aid training let me. Before long I had to deal with an injury on the quay where a docker had been knocked down by a bogie which was a battery powered flat platform cart. The ambulance was called and all I could do was reassure him that help was on its way. He was still conscious and when the ambulance arrived the medic asked his name and he replied "Heenan". I realised and informed the medic that they docker was giving him the name of the East Ham solicitor who would deal with his claim! When he recovered, the docker did make that claim and got his payout.

I'd been going out with Pauline for a while when one evening at her flat she informed me she was pregnant. To be honest I wasn't ready, but I did love her and said I'd sort everything out. We eventually told our parents and they all agreed we should get married as soon as possible so we booked a church in Forest Gate. In the meantime, I found a flat to rent in Cann Hall Road, Leytonstone for two pounds and fifteen shillings a week. It was a downstairs flat in a house like the one Pauline had grown up in. The only difference being that this one had an inside toilet. It didn't have a bath which was hard for me as I loved to have a bath so went out and bought a tin one but didn't really enjoy it as much. We got the rest of our furniture from a nearby second-hand store.

We got married a few weeks later and all my mates from the docks came to the reception in Barking and had a lovely time. We got home at midnight with all our gifts and flopped on the bed and into a deep sleep.

The next morning my new wife made a nice breakfast which I hadn't had for a long time. We then opened our gifts and counted the money from our cards. We'd done well. We didn't have a honeymoon as the baby was due soon, so I was back at work the following day, listening to stories about the reception.

A lot of dockers had second jobs, mostly those who couldn't get on a regular gang. You'd see some coming into work driving the taxi's they ran outside the docks. We were now on a shift system of seven until two and two until nine, which suited me. A friend asked if I wanted some gardening work in Chigwell on the side and I agreed and so would drive to Stradbroke Drive to help him out when I wasn't on shift. The going rate was about seven shillings an hour so I'd usually get a pound for three hours' work. After I'd finished one afternoon, I was walking back to my car when a woman called out, asking if I did any window cleaning. I said I did but had no ladder or sponge. It turned out she only wanted the bottom ones done and though I'd never done any window cleaning before in my life I was there for over an hour and when I went to get paid I just asked for whatever the usual cleaner would get. As I was leaving, a Pink Mini came onto the driveway and the woman driver gave me a funny glance. I realised then who she was, and that I'd just finished cleaning Bobby Moore's windows!

Also, one day around this time there was a buzz around the docks about a horse called Horseradish, running at one of the courses that day. A lot of the men put money on it and I decided to put five pounds on. Later that day a huge cheer went up as the news came in that Horseradish had won and cost the local bookie over two hundred pounds which left him in a real state. I'm not a gambling man but thought I'd chance my luck that day so I put some of my winnings on a couple of dogs running later that evening. I had a winner there as well and was able to give my dad some money the next day. He told me not to give any of it back to the bookies and I've stood by that since then. Even now I must really think before putting a bet on the Grand National.

Back in Cann Hall Road my wife had given up work and was keeping house. She often saw her parents who lived nearby, and her sister Frances also visited occasionally. Our landlord's name was Mr Fisher and he always came for the rent at six o'clock on a Friday evening. We always complained about the damp patches in the flat, but he took no notice. A typical landlord.

My daughter was born on twenty-ninth of October and we named her Jane Anne. We were both very proud and I thought it was time I applied for a mortgage, so we could get a house. We applied to the Greater London Council wo were giving one hundred percent mortgages at the time and after about two months I was given one and found a house in East Ham. We moved into 22 Swinburn Avenue in the January and it was a real improvement on where we'd come from. It was three-bedroom with a thirty-two foot through lounge and large kitchen. It also a large cellar, a bathroom and a lovely bath. On the first night we got in the bath together!

Shortly after we'd moved in a few friends visited for a party and when I told them how we'd got the mortgage they said they would try their luck too. We soon furnished the place, using Williams, a furniture store in East Ham High Street. We had plenty of time to get all the things we needed, but I really had to get a mower as the back garden was very long and mainly laid to lawn. We planned to stay forever.

Back in the docks I was getting good work some weeks but not as much as I'd have liked. One of the ships we unloaded was Japanese and came in quite often. One of our gang was always missing when it did, and I found out from a friend that he was exempt due to being a prisoner of war in one of the Japanese camps, so there was no knowing what he'd do, especially if he'd had a few drinks.

I always found the crews very friendly, as were the Chinese ships. If you went into their lounge you'd find them playing games with counters and they sometimes came onto the quay with little red books to give out, on the teachings of Mao.

Around this time, I organised a beano for my gang one Saturday, with some others from different gangs. About fourteen of us in all were picked up by minibus early that day and went off to Zeebrugge for a few drinks and some fun. Once we were on the ferry the pints started flowing despite it being a rough crossing and when we got to the town square there was a band playing. They finished up, thanked everyone and went into a nearby bar. I suggested that was the place to go as the beer must be cheap and was right. There was a small stage inside, with a woman singing and once she'd finished I grabbed the microphone and did a couple of my own, much to the amusement of our group!

I made a beeline for the band leader and asked if he wanted a whisky, to which he readily agreed. I made sure I got him a double and got chatting to him. In the end I bought him three doubles as I wondered how he'd perform when they went back out to play! Come the time he could hardly stand up and I told the band I'd take his place as I knew how to use a baton. By now our group were in fits of laughter but wanted to see what would happen next. I'd had quite a bit to drink but soon began to sober up when I was outside, in public leading the band. I managed to last about ten minutes and thought I was doing well until someone came and gently took the baton out of my hand. I'll never forget that afternoon and the fun we had on the beano. After about five hours it was time to return to the ferry and we were still drinking on the crossing back home. Our group were falling asleep one after the other, but I was still hyperactive and off looking for more fun and games. I got waylaid by a group in orange outfits and realised they were Hare Krishna people who were trying to convert me. They'd been to a convention and tried their luck in getting me to think the same way they did, but they had no chance. By now I was the only one of my group still awake and kept the other passengers amused by balancing empty coke cans on my colleague's heads. I fact I was placing the cans everywhere I could balance them. When we got back to port, and they started to wake up all the cans and other things I'd found started falling off and it was the main topic of conversation on the following Monday. In fact, I think it started a trend that carried on with other beanos.

Things were going well at home in Swinburn Avenue. Our little Jane wasn't giving us many sleepless nights and my wife's parents were a great help. My own father hadn't yet visited though he'd seen Jane when we went to visit him in Hainault shortly after the birth. I remember when taking my wife to the hospital when the baby was due. The doctor asked what I did for a living and seemed impressed as I was there all suited and booted so suggested it would be a good idea for me to wait in his office instead of the waiting room. I accepted, and he said someone would bring me in a cup of tea. About half an hour later the doctor came back and said my wife should be giving birth very soon. We got chatting again and he asked if I worked in a surgery or hospital. I was confused and asked what he meant, and he replied that I'd told him I was a doctor. I said I wasn't a doctor, but in fact a docker which made him change his tune and I was soon back in the waiting room! It wasn't my fault he hadn't understood my accent.

There was a man called Arthur Easter who lived in Branch Road at this time. He got me out of trouble on a couple of occasions, once a few years earlier when I skidded my bike into a garden fence opposite where he lived. He came across and told me to get off home, and he'd sort things out with the woman who lived there. When I went back the following day the repairs had all been done by Arthur. Sadly, he is no longer with us, but my friend Frank Coot went to the funeral and said there was a big turnout. He was a wonderful man.

When one of our gang went on holiday they gave us a replacement who someone referred to as 'the ghost'. When I asked why he was called this, one of the gang replied that he was a shadow of his former self, and when I saw him walking towards us I realised why. He was as white as a sheet and would scare the hell out of you if you saw him on a dark night in nothing but his underpants!

This brings me on to nicknames. My nickname in the docks was '008' as I had the dock number 0008 which I must have got when someone retired. There was 'Smokey' who'd been fined several times for smoking on dock premises and 'Sleepy Time Joe' who would be working away normally and suddenly fall asleep, sometimes when driving a fork lift truck. I think there's a medical diagnosis for that nowadays.

We also had a man called 'Buckets of Blood' as even the smallest cut would bleed profusely, and a crane driver known as 'The Gannet', who was as skinny as a rake but could eat anything and did. One morning I saw him take up the crane seven pound of corned beef and when he came down at the end of the shift the tin was empty. Then he went for his dinner.

There was another called 'Jimmy Sideways' as he always spoke out of one side of his mouth and it seemed to go right up to his cheekbone. We could be very cruel. One man was called 'Nuts and Bolts' because he always picking up loose screws and washers and the like.

One day my van wouldn't start so I had to go to work without it. When it came to the end of the shift I was asking around to see who could give me a lift home and was told that 'Spit and Gob' was on the quay and went the same way. I wondered why he had that nickname but didn't have long to find out. He seemed like a nice, jolly fellow and agreed to give me a lift home so when we were on the way, we were chatting, and he suddenly made a throaty noise, his head twitched and looked over his shoulder as he spat into the back of his car. I was just thankful I was sitting beside him and wondered what his house must be like. He didn't have many friends, and certainly no followers!

I'd also seen a man walking round looking skywards in the docks and asked my friend who he was. He told me he worked sweeping up the warehouses and said his wife had run off with an airline pilot, and he'd been looking for her ever since! The reality was that poor man had an accident on the quay and was put on light duty. As I said, we could be a cruel lot, but no harm was meant.

Chapter Thirteen

Moving On

I came home to Swinburn Avenue one day and my wife handed me a letter that stated our house was to be compulsorily purchased to make way for a school. In fact, about five streets were being demolished. I was shocked as the searches had all been done when we bought the place, but nothing had come up. Still, there was nothing we could do.

To top it all, we owed the GLC more than we'd bought the house for and they wouldn't give us another mortgage as they only lent to first-time buyers. Newham Council would pay the mortgage and give us expenses for moving so we quickly had to find somewhere new to live. We panicked a bit but managed to get a mortgage on a three-bedroomed house in Chadwin Road, Plaistow. It was a small place and only had a back yard with a shed in it. In fact, the yard was only about a yard long! It meant that you could put your legs out of the back door for about two hours when it was sunny then turn around and get your face and chest tanned.

The good thing about it was the location. Only two miles from the docks and the same to my Aunt's place in Canning Town. The father of Terry Spinks, a famous boxer, lived a few doors away and always stopped for a chat.

Still, we never felt settled and weren't happy there. As well, some of the ships were now stopping at Tilbury Container Port instead of coming down to the Royal Docks so there was less work available. But finally, we had some luck when we decided to sell and managed to get double what we'd paid for the place just nine months later. We started looking around Chadwell Heath and although property was expensive we were able to get a Maisonette for about ten thousand pounds.

We moved in and were happier than we'd been in a long time. There was a nearby school and some shops, as well as being a short bus ride from Romford Market and Ilford. Another good thing about it was that I'd managed to get some part-time work in nearby Chigwell, doing things like painting and decorating. We'd been in the new place for about five months when my wife fell pregnant again and I was over the moon. We were hoping for a boy but really didn't mind providing the baby was healthy.

I was still working in the docks, but it was about a thirty-minute drive and though our gang was usually lucky there were times when we had no work, which was when my part-time jobs came in handy. I remember walking to the newsagents one morning and saw a family being evicted. I told my wife when I got home and a few weeks later we saw it was up for sale and asked for a viewing. It had no central heating and needed a lot of decorating, but we liked it and our bid was accepted. We quickly sold the Maisonette and moved into 29 Grove Road, Chadwell Heath, hoping it would be our last move. It was a nice neighbourhood with plenty of shops and everything else you needed nearby.

I had to get my finger out and start decorating but it was our first night there, so I went to bed and after a while heard a lot of shouting and swearing. I looked out of the window and saw a man ripping the gate off the post. Someone must have phoned the police as they were outside by the time I'd got dressed and gone outside. It turned out the man was the one who'd been evicted a few months earlier and seemed very drunk. I didn't press charges as I was planning to remove the lot that weekend to make a driveway. Although the police told him not to come back, he slept in a nearby phone box that night.

We soon got working central heating and I gave the rooms a lick of paint which made it much more comfortable. The back garden was also a bit of a state, so I had my work cut out, but it was everything we needed, with three bedrooms and some good-sized rooms. Our new baby was born on the twenty first of May 1971 and we named her Jo Anne. My wife's parents were first on the scene and I was glad about that. Again, my father was a no-show, but he never really got involved in our lives and I think he was oblivious of what was going on around him most of the time.

The Grove Social Club was over the road from our house and I joined so I could occasionally pop over for a drink. I was working a lot and though we weren't rich we had enough to get by. I never bought much on hire purchase and if I did it was paid up before we bought anything else. The man who ripped the gate off never did come back and I later found out he was often drunk and didn't pay the mortgage, as well as being violent towards his wife. The club, being so close, was probably too much temptation for him.

I'd also joined the Scruttons Social Club outside Victoria Docks where I was based at the time. We were to have some fantastic evenings there. I used to go there with my wife and some friends of ours, Sheila and Johnny Hoadley. One night we went to see Karl Denver who sang songs such as Wimoweh, Mexicali Rose and China Doll. We were walking to the club and I saw a posh car with a man sitting in the back seat, who turned out to be Karl. Being the joker, I tapped on the window and when he looked up in a drunken state I said, 'you're on soon Karl'. He put his thumb up as if to say, 'I'm ready'. Once we were in the club and had got our table, Karl walked in and got a drink from the bar. He gave us a fantastic evening despite the amount he'd knocked back. We had many nights out with Sheila and Johnny and usually resulted in us ending up back at theirs for a cup of tea and a sandwich.

In the mid-seventies a man moved in to a house a few doors down from us. His name was Peter Craven and he'd come from the East End with his wife Rita, a lovely lady. The first time we went over to the social club it was a great night and we must have put away quite a few beers. I recall my wife not being so happy about this.

By now our children were settled in school and doing things like taking swimming lessons. We had another new neighbour who I through I recognised. When we got chatting he said he remembered throwing me off his parents' smallholding on Five Oaks Lane many years before. His name was Christopher Fryer and he was to become a good friend. I introduced Christopher to Peter and we went over to the social club together. Soon, my new friends went into business together and we spent many more evenings in the social club, but my wife wasn't happy with the amount of time I was over there though I made sure they never went short. I was working hard and felt I deserved a social life but suppose I was being a bit neglectful.

My father had recently taken voluntary redundancy from the docks and was offered three thousand, five hundred pounds. I told him not to accept it, but he said he'd never seen that much money in his life so was taking it. He got a job in a paint factory on the Hainault Industrial Estate and hated it, though I did warn him about working bell to bell.

I got a transfer to Tilbury Container Port at this time as the Port of London was shutting down and this was to be the principal port in the east of England, located further along the River Thames in Essex. There were general cargo ships and every few weeks a log ship but best of all were the roll-on roll-off ships where you drove cars on to them. I joined a gang run by Freddie Harris who I think was from Benfleet. He was a likeable chap and loved deep-sea fishing, and had a boat moored in Westcliff, near Southend. I settled in quickly and stayed in that gang for the rest of my time in the docks. The wages were better on the container and ro-ro ships than on the log ships which I didn't enjoy working on. Some of the logs were over thirty-foot-long and there were a lot of accidents. I was able to pass a course to drive a forty-ton fork-lift truck which lifted the logs, and this meant a bit more money in my pocket. There was also a social club in the docks where I joined the darts team and had some good times.

When I was on a late shift I'd take my eldest daughter to school or do a bit of work in Chigwell, mostly gardening. One day when I was doing this a Jewish man came up and asked if I did any painting. I said I did and he told me he had some flats in Ilford that needed doing so I agreed to go and look at them. His name was Mr Abraham.

Gardening work was back breaking, and I didn't like doing it in the winter months so about a week later I went to look at the work he wanted me to do and agreed but said it could only be done when I'd finished my shifts in the docks. I didn't make much money, but it was out of the cold and rain. Mr Abraham also let out rooms in housed at about forty pounds a week but got around the renting laws by changing the sheets once a week and having the room hoovered so it was classed as a hotel. I don't know how he got away with it.

One day I was working in one of these houses, in Eastwood Road, Goodmayes when I had to knock on the door of one of the rented rooms. It was opened by a man called Fred who q me in to check the work that needed doing. I told him I'd be back in a week and when I returned I knocked on the door again to be greeted by Fred, dressed in women's clothes. I'd seen it all before on the ships but quickly said I needed to go back to the office to make a call. I phoned Mr Abraham who told me that Fred had been in that week and informed them he wanted to be called Frederica, and his tenancy agreement altered. Mr Abraham refused and that was that. I went back to the room and did the work but was glad to get out of there.

A few months later I was doing some work in a young woman's room on a lower floor in the house and asked her what she thought of Fred upstairs. She replied that Fred always spoke to her, but his mum didn't. I told her it was Fred dressed up and a few weeks later told me I was right. She couldn't believe things like that went on. My wife also saw him dressed up, walking into the ladies' toilets in Chadwell Heath.

Back in Grove Road, Chris Fryer opened a yard at the end of the road called 'Fryers Tyres'. I helped him get all the equipment into the building and he was soon in business.

I'd been working at Tilbury for about nine months and was enjoying it, though I couldn't get bread and dripping or beef sandwiches I'd enjoyed at Victoria Docks. I still enjoyed working on the ro-ro ships as our gang was guaranteed the work, because we could all drive. On one ship we worked, there was an army jeep stowed sideways as there was no more space. One of my friends was trying to drive it off, going backwards and forwards and doing a lot of damage. In the end it came down the ramp looking a bit worse for wear and an army man standing nearby said it had seen more action in the last ten minutes than in the sixty years it was in the Sudan. I asked where it was going to and he said it was destined for a museum but wasn't sure what would happen to it now.

I loved loading the ro-ro ships as I could have my pick of the vehicles being driven on. I was the only one who wanted to drive the fire-engines, ambulances, lorries and even the odd tank. I also drove a few bubble cars and three wheelers on. It was more like a day out than a job.

One morning we were working on a ship with general cargo and one of my mates opened a box full of whisky, to try it out for taste. I also had a drop and must admit it was very nice, so had a few slugs before the shift ended. I was driving home when a policeman on a motorbike pulled me over and asked to see my documents. He said I'd been speeding and asked me why I was going so fast. I told him I wanted to get home as my wife was ill, so he wished her well and told me to drive on and be careful. I couldn't believe the conversation had happened and told my wife and friends. It was only a few weeks later in the docks we were discussing car insurance and I showed my friend my documents. He said I needed to get it altered as it stated my occupation as 'Doctor'. I realised then why the policeman had let me go despite me speeding and probably being over the limit. It was the second time a miss-spelling of 'Docker' had done me a favour.

I'd been working at Tilbury for a few years when we were asked if we wanted to take voluntary redundancy, with eight thousand, five hundred pounds being offered. I mulled it over for a few weeks and thought it was a good sum of money so applied. I left the docks with my money and had a party in the social club. I still had mixed feelings and wondered if I'd done the right thing. I hadn't. The docks were the best time of my working life and even worse, a few weeks later the offer was increased to thirty-eight thousand pounds.

In all the time I worked there, I don't think I ever actually went into Tilbury Town. However, I was to get to know it much better in years to come.

Chapter Fourteen

The Milkman and the Tower Bridge Tour Guide

Now I've left the docks and though I have my redundancy pay I'm feeling down and must find a new job. I've a couple of weeks off and during this time I buy Pauline a car as she's been having driving lessons. A few weeks earlier I'd had a few drinks with the family in Scruttons Club by the docks and was on my way home when I stupidly overtook a taxi on a zebra crossing. Further down the road I was pulled over by the police. The officer asked if I'd been drinking and I said I had. I had to sit in the police car and he handed me the dreaded breathalyser. When I'd done the test, he told me I'd failed and was over the limit. His colleague wanted to arrest me but as my children were in the car they told us to walk the rest of the way home, which was about ten minutes. This was a real wakeup call for me and I've never done anything like it since. I happened to see the same policeman on school crossing duty the next day and thanked him.

We went on a family outing that weekend to John Lewis and bought a large Chaise Longue for the front room. We had a bit of a spend up that day and when I got home I spotted an advert in the local paper. United Dairies were recruiting milkmen for their depot in London Road, Chadwell Heath. I applied and was taken on, starting the following Monday. I was looking forward to working in the open air and didn't mind that I had to be at the depot at five in the morning as I was always up early, even on Sundays. On the Monday morning I went to the depot and met with Mike, who was going to teach me the ropes. My round included Whalebone Lane in Chadwell Heath and then onto the Marks Gate Estate which was built on farmland in the fifties and sixties because of the overflow of houses in Dagenham.

I'd always been told it was a good estate, but I was only to last about nine months there. I started in the middle of winter with Mike and soon got into the flow. I was told that everything must be put into the book and on the Friday when I knocked on doors asking for payment, most did so but some told me they'd see me the following week. They still asked for butter, potatoes, bread and even the odd chicken. After two weeks I started doing the rounds on my own and things were going well. I made sure everything was put down in the book and when I got back to the depot everything I brought back was counted off the milk float.

When I collected the money a lot of the women wanted to gossip about their neighbours and some thought they were doing you a favour by paying in coins which I hated as I had to count it all out again when handing in the money for the day. On a good day I finished around eleven in the morning, so I could still do my part-time work.

Sometimes when I got back to the depot I'd be ten or so bottles short and I think they were being stolen whilst I was delivering to the high-rise flats, and there were always families who didn't pay up, but the Dairy just wrote the bills off. I even had the odd offer of payment in kind from some of the women which I didn't take them up on! But after about nine months I found I didn't enjoy the job and the stress that came with it.

I decided to leave United Dairies and take a short break. I soon saw an advert for a tour guide on Tower Bridge and phoned for an application form. I filled it out and was invited for interview. A week later I was on the payroll for the Corporation of London. The Tower Bridge Walkways were to be reopened to the public for the first time since 1912. They'd been closed all that time because of the thieving and prostitution that went on.

There were about ten of us tourist guides. We'd been given books to read about the Bridge and surrounding areas, and the job was to go up on the walkways and talk to people about it all. On the day of the opening, Princess Margaret arrived for the ceremony, cut the tape and declared the walkways open. My job on the day was to let the balloons off but it had gone wrong and instead of going up individually they all got tangled up and went up in three bunches. To make matters worse there were free entry tickets tied to each balloon, so someone was going to have hundreds of tickets.

We were told to always be polite and if we were asked a question we didn't know the answer to, we had to talk our way out of it. After a few months of working alongside each other we'd have a bit of a laugh and though the pay wasn't great it was a living wage. We did have a few perks, such as going on HMS Belfast, the old warship moored alongside the bridge. We were allowed in the Mess Room for a pint at lunch time and could also go into the Beefeaters Bar on Tower Pier.

One day an American couple asked if I had a twin who worked on the other walkway. I said I did, but he was just going off duty! Another American asked if Charles Dickens drank in the nearby Dickens Inn pub. I told him he did but wouldn't be in until three. Another day, I was standing outside the bridge entrance when a young Swedish woman came up and said 'hi', so I replied 'hi' and she asked, "what you say, I whip you?". I asked what for and she replied to really hurt you, strangle and kill you. I realised what she meant and pointed her in the direction of the London Dungeons!

I soon found a way of earning a little extra cash by telling people with expensive cameras that I could take them to places on the bridge where the public were not allowed so they could get better photos. For a small charge of course.

Then one evening I got a call about a decorating job in Wanstead that would last about five weeks, so I decided to hand my notice in and become self-employed. The Tower Bridge job had given me some good times and friends, and I still have great memories of the place.

Chapter Fifteen

Going it Alone

I'd given a lot of thought to working for myself as a decorator as I knew a lot of people in Ilford and the surrounding areas on the lookout for tradesmen. Many of them were Jewish and I'd already worked on a lot of houses along Manor Road in Chigwell, including for a certain Mr Eves who is better known for Bairstow Eves, the Estate Agents chain with offices throughout England.

I bought a new van and work stated coming in. The money wasn't great, but I could choose my hours and the jobs I'd take on. This allowed me family time and we were able to take the girls out to lots of different places. One evening we were all in Scruttons Club and on stage was Jim Bowen, of Bullseye fame, doing a one-man show. I got to talk to him afterwards, but he seemed a bit grumpy!

Over the next few years I built up my business and family life continued as normal. My friends Peter and Chris Fryer went into business together around this time. I was in Chadwell Heath one morning when I met up with an old friend from the docks, John Boyd. He'd left the Royal Docks some years before to become a plasterer and was living locally so I promised to get him work. John could put his hand to anything including bricklaying and woodwork, but one thing he couldn't do was read.

The Grove Social Club was a magnet for Peter, Chris and me on a Friday evening and we'd be propping up the bar every week. Soon we were drinking after hours, getting home about three in the morning and I knew my wife was getting fed up with it.

I got a call from one of my clients asking if I wanted to take on a big job with my mate John in Bow, just off Stratford Broadway. It was converting a Mortuary into a fashion warehouse. We met him a few days later at the place to find out what needed doing and when we arrived all the bodies had white sheets over them, including some small ones that must have been children.

The place was being emptied and the work needed to start in a couple of weeks' time, so we agreed and got John's son Steve in to help us, as well as a couple of other people. When we started, the client, Mr Cedar, came down with a few pages of what he wanted done and there was no contract as we'd worked for him before and he knew we wouldn't take him on, money-wise. We had to get rid of the slabs and sinks, and about thirty coffins of which one was solid oak. We tried to get buyers for them but the only two people who turned up wanted the oak coffin. One as a motorcycle sidecar and the other for a drinks cabinet!

We also had piles of shrouds, rolls of coffin velvet, crosses and coffin handles but nobody wanted any of it. There was an iron outlet pipe at the ground floor entrance and when I stood under it and gave it a whack with a hammer to dislodge it, the pipe split open spilling congealed blood everywhere, mainly over me. I had a quick shower and put on some new overalls but will never forget that experience. Eventually we got rid of the coffins in a large skip. The driver looked on in amazement as we loaded them on and said he couldn't take them, but we insisted we'd paid so he had to. Eventually, after about a month the showroom was ready and handed over to a very pleased Mr Cedar.

We were glad to get away from Bow as it wasn't a nice area. While we were working there we had a tramp come banging on the door asking for money for food, and there were a lot of muggings going on. I went around the back of the building on one day and saw about twenty purses and wallets on the floor, so called the police.

We earned well out of that job (I don't mean the wallets!) and one night soon after I'd had a lovely meal and some wine with my wife. We were lying in bed and heard a loud noise. A car had crashed into the back of my car outside and I'd only bought it a few weeks earlier. I quickly got into my pyjamas and ran outside but by then the car had reversed and started to drive away, slowing down to let a woman out before carrying on. The woman was running away so I called out to my wife to phone the police and gave chase. I caught up with her at the end of Grove Road and she turned and accused me of being from the nearby hospital and being a nuisance to her. The police arrived and took her down to the station. Later on, they caught her boyfriend who was drunk. I got the insurance details and filed a claim, but it wasn't going to be easy to get paid out as a few weeks before the same man had another accident and the car was a write-off but let him drive it for the last two months of his insurance without any repairs being carried out.

The night he hit my car he only had two days insurance left and the company started fobbing me off with excuses. After a few weeks of this I'd had enough and took my family down to their offices in South Woodford. We were in reception and I told the clerk I wanted the money for my car, but they refused so I said I wouldn't be leaving until they did. They threatened to call the police and have us removed but I said they should do and call the Daily Mirror while they were at it.

Eventually another clerk came out and promised us a cheque within a couple of days and I replied that if we didn't get it then I'd be back with even more of my family. Aunts, uncles and everyone! The next day a claims assessor came to look over the car and three days later I got a cheque for three-hundred and twenty pounds.

Soon after this incident we went away to the Costa Brava for a couple of weeks and had a lovely time. The place wasn't so busy as it is nowadays. When we got back home I wondered what messages I'd have on my answerphone about upcoming work but there were none. We were entering a bit of a recession and I would only get the occasional job from Mr Abraham who needed a driver to take him in his Daimler to various meetings. I didn't mind this as it was a few pounds in the pocket.

By now both my daughters were pupils at Chadwell Heath High School, only a stones throw away from our house. My wife had a cleaning job there, but I didn't have much work and we were just about getting by. As I was always out with my friends on a Friday night at the Grove Social Club my wife said she was going to start meeting up with a friend of hers, with the children which I was pleased about as she could have a bit of a social life as well.

One Friday night we'd had a good evening and were leaving the club when Chris Fryer said he'd locked his keys inside his house, opposite the club. I decided to climb up the drainpipe and get in by the open window, and there was now a crowd outside watching this drunken man climbing the pipe and cheering me on. It was about midnight and probably didn't go down too well with the neighbours. I finally managed to get in and open the door, delivering my good deed for the night. But I needed to visit the doctor on Monday morning as I'd given myself a bad back!

At the doctors I was the first patient and the receptionist told me to wait for him to arrive. After about half an hour I was told to go into the room and waited in there for another fifteen minutes before I went back to ask the receptionist where he was. She told me he'd been taken ill but would be back soon so to go back in and wait, which I did. He came back shortly afterwards and apologised for being late. He then started crying and told me he'd just come back to work after a nervous breakdown. I'm not sure why but I just asked what had triggered it all off and he told me he had a good home life and came in to do the morning surgery, then locum calls and minor operations in the local hospital in the afternoons before coming back in for the early evening surgery. I said this workload was no good for him and he should cut down if he wanted to feel better. He thanked me and agreed he would do that, before asking what was wrong with me. I said not to worry about me and just look after himself before I left. I don't think he took my advice as he committed suicide about a year later.

A few days later I got a letter from the Grove Social Club informing me I'd been barred for three months for what they termed 'hanging from the guttering of a house opposite the club at midnight and making noise'. I didn't know you could get barred for that but found another club close by that belonged to the PLA. It was a large building with a field behind where they played rugby. We were made very welcome at the club and they even tried to get Peter to join the rugby team. It was a good thing that we got a cab to the club as most of our new friends there were Port of London Police. We had many good evenings there including fancy dress nights and I remember one occasion when I went as a judge and Peter as a pirate.

Back at Grove Road my wife would leave the children with me on a Saturday morning and go to the markets with her friend. I started doing some decorating work around this time in Wanstead, for a woman called Mrs Roxburgh, whose husband was Professor Ian Roxburgh. They were a lovely couple to work for and I recall wallpapering their hallway, stairwells and landing that went up three floors, using more than thirty rolls of paper. It took about a month with all the preparation and painting involved.

One morning I was at home and the children were at school. I said to my wife that I knew something was wrong between us and she started to cry, admitting that she was seeing another man. Naturally it really hurt me and though we did try to make our marriage work for the next few months we were still rowing, and it wasn't working out, so she moved out and filed for divorce. My daughters stayed with me as Jane was near to leaving school and we didn't want the upheaval of moving Jo-Anne away from her friends. It was hard work looking after two daughters and holding down a job, but we made the best of it and I took them to see my father and his partner Betty who had moved from Hainault to a block of flats in Bow called Albert Big Point. I had tears in my eyes when I told my father that that Pauline and I were divorcing but he just said I should never cry over a woman and he'd disown me if I did.

When we left I just felt he was a hard man with no compassion and didn't speak to him for many years afterwards. Betty would put up with a lot in the coming years.

I said to Jane that I was sorry we were a one parent family, but she said a few of her friends were in the same position and they still got to see their mother as much as they could.

One evening shortly after this there was a knock at the door and when I answered it there was a young lad from across the road asking if I could lend him a fiver, so he could go to football training at West Ham. That lad was Paul Ince and I'm still waiting for that fiver back!

The next few months were a hard slog as there wasn't a lot of money coming in and I must keep an eye on my girls, but every Tuesday night a couple of my friends would come around to my house to play country music and have a few beers. These were good times that took my mind off a lot of the sorrow I was going through. I went on a dating site and met a couple of women, but it wasn't really for me. I even met a woman who moved in with her three daughters, but it only lasted a few months.

Can you imagine, five teenage girls in the house and boys hanging around outside every night?

We were back to square one with just me and the girls. I would soon be getting divorced and the house would be up for sale, so we decided the girls should go to live with their mother. I put the house on the market and managed to get a few good jobs so decided it would be a good time to visit my sister who lived in Hawaii near Lahaina Beach on the island of Maui. I booked the flight to Los Angeles from Gatwick and the connection to Honolulu, and on to Maui. I think it came to about eight hundred pounds for the air fare, so my credit card helped me out. The flight to Los Angeles was about twelve hours and got off to an interesting start shortly after take-off when the plane did just about everything except loop-the-loop. Some passengers were screaming, and the pilot came on the intercom saying he'd never experienced a take-off quite like it!

We made it to Los Angeles and I had to wait for a couple of hours for the plane to Honolulu. When I boarded the stewardess said I could sit wherever I wanted as there were only seven passengers and I think I ended up talking to most of them to pass the time. We landed in the early evening and were told the last plane to Maui had left and the next would be the following morning, so I had to get a hotel for the night.

I got to Maui the next morning after a short journey, looking out over the islands and wonderful beaches. I was met by my sister Rita and her boyfriend as she'd now divorced from her husband Ray. They put garlands round my neck as is the traditional greeting and drove me out to their Condo about five miles from the airport. It was about ten in the morning and the heat was already unbearable.

Over the next two weeks they took me to the rain forest, on crater hikes and the dazzling waterfalls and beaches. One day I was sunbathing on the beach when I felt the ground move and my sister confirmed to me later they'd had a minor earthquake as they got them now and again. It was during this holiday saw a shopping mall for the first time and couldn't believe how big it was. I bought a few country music cassettes there for me and my friends to listen to when I got home, and my sister also taped the Country Music Awards for me to take back. We had some good times and lovely meals in restaurants as well as home-cooked dinners. But the time went quickly, and I was soon on my way home to an empty house, wondering what life had in store for me.

When I got home I switched on my answerphone and there was a message from a Mr Hanson, a friend of Mr Cedar asking if I'd be interested in doing a conversion in a factory with a mezzanine floor, for pharmaceutical products. I met him the following day, taking John with me and we agreed a daily rate plus completion bonus. He wanted a mezzanine floor with two toilet blocks and a white room where staff were to count tablets. John and his son Steve could turn their hand to anything and were good to have but we needed a carpenter so put an advert in the paper for one, at a rate of £100 per day. We also recruited a roofer called Peter Wilson who was from Dagenham.

We got a call from a carpenter and told him to meet us on Monday at the site. When he showed up John asked where his tools were, but he only had a hammer and saw. I think John took pity on him and gave him the job anyway. I turned out he'd come from Ireland looking for work and his real job was a jockey. He was only five-foot tall. Luckily, John had all the tools needed so we got to work on cleaning up the factory. You wouldn't believe the rubbish left behind when premises are vacated but we got on with it and finished the job in about six weeks.

I suggested to John that we have a break in Spain and though he'd never been on a plane before and feared flying he agreed, as long as his wife didn't mind. We ended up having a lovely time in Costa Brava and I didn't have anyone telling me when I should stop drinking!

I had a few jobs lined up when I got home so life was looking up a bit, but the house still hadn't been sold. The following Monday I received a letter from the Inland Revenue requesting me to attend their office in Gants Hill on the Wednesday morning. I wondered what it was all about but was soon to find out. On the Tuesday evening I had my usual night with my friends and some country music. They also brought round some brochures for Nashville, Tennessee as they were planning to go and wanted me to come along. I said I'd look as I fancied another holiday. Why not? I was a single man now.

Chapter Sixteen

A visit to the Tax Office and a New Start

On the Wednesday morning I went to the tax office where I was ushered into a room by two men who showed me my tax returns for the previous few years and asked if they were correct. When I replied they were, one of the men said I'd earned about eight thousand pounds over the last three years. I claimed I hadn't earned a lot as I was a single parent. Then they played their trump card, with one claiming he couldn't afford a holiday abroad on his wages but I just replied that it wasn't my fault if he didn't earn enough. But I knew what they were getting at.

The man said he'd always wanted to go to Spain and I suggested he started saving up, but they cut to the chase and said "let's talk about Hawaii and the three holiday's you've had this year. How can you afford it?". I claimed that most of it was on my credit card. This wasn't getting us anywhere, so they asked to visit my house, and I agreed.

When they arrived, they noticed the Jaguar car on my driveway which looked good but to be honest was on its last legs. When inside they also noticed the brochures for Nashville. This wasn't going well. They asked where my safe was, but I didn't have one, so they went around the house and told me to come back to their office the following week.

On the Saturday I went to a country music festival and met a woman called Barbara who was from Tilbury in Essex. Then the following week it was back to the tax office where I was told they'd looked over everything and calculated I owed the Inland Revenue forty thousand pounds. I asked which floor of the building we were on as I might as well jump now. I didn't believe I owed anything like that and couldn't pay it, so they suggested we negotiate though I didn't know if I could with them. After a little while they suggested three thousand pounds, so I quickly agreed and wrote a cheque for the full amount. They wondered how I was able to pay straight away and I told them I'd just had a good job and an accountant, so I wouldn't get in this situation again. The country was in a recession, but my good friend Peter Craven lent me the money. He knew he'd get it back as I had found a buyer for my house.

I carried on seeing Barbara and when the house was sold I rented a flat in Tilbury to be nearer to her. She kindly agreed to look after my LPs and other things of value. I needed to find work and saw an advert in the paper for security guards at the Nat West Tower in Bishopsgate, after it'd been bombed by the IRA. I started and after some training was on site for 12 hour shifts which were a killer and some of the other guards didn't stay for long. The job consisted of walking up and around all forty-two floors, some of which had key stations where you had to register you were there. All the windows had been blown out by the bomb, so it was really open to the elements, and in the basement, you could see the twisted beams where the building had jumped two feet!

It was tiring with all the walking and the boredom got on my nerves so found a new hobby – collecting pens. When the bomb went off it created a vacuum that twirled everything in the building around no matter how heavy it was. Items were scattered all over the place and there were some lovely pens lying around. I wasn't stealing as they were destined for the skip for some reason. I stayed for about nine months but had to quit because of leg-ache. I moved on to another security job with Silver Wings Security at Lincoln's Inn Fields, working in a building that housed six law offices. Barristers and Lawyers were coming into the building all the time and my job was to see to all the passes. I also did night shifts as some of the meetings went on late and when they were finished the office staff would bring down the leftover food for us, which was some of the best you could buy. The work was quite interesting as there was a lot of gossip about who was carrying on with who, and a secure room that held all the paperwork for the upcoming Maxwell trial. But I was offered a job by another security firm in Thurrock for the same money but with less travel costs, so I took it and started at DSL, a holding warehouse for Marks & Spencer. It was also better because I was nearer to my girlfriend Barbara and was now living with her and her son and daughter.

I found out that DSL were recruiting and told Barbara who also got a job there. As well as looking after all my LPs, including my Johnny Cash collection, Barbara adopted my cat, Tansy. I eventually moved in and had some good times there. One I must mention is when a local takeaway advertised the 'hottest ever pizza'. I thought I'd have some of that as I loved hot and spicy food, so phoned up one evening to order. When it arrived, I took a bit or two out of the first slice and was disappointed. I'd had hotter pizzas than this and didn't find it very spicy at all, so I phoned them back to complain. They said they'd send round a replacement free of charge and it turned up about twenty minutes later. This time, when I opened the box you could almost feel the heat coming off it. I couldn't get near it, let alone eat it so it promptly went into the bin and I finished off the first one. They'd obviously taken my complaint badly and given me a radioactive pizza!

I mentioned earlier that I'd been to a country music festival and really enjoyed these. I once went to a festival in Peterborough to see Tom T Hall, also known as the Storyteller. Tom's most famous song was 'Old Dogs and Children and Watermelon Wine'. On the day of the show I asked the receptionist of the hotel we were staying at where the most expensive hotel in Peterborough was and suggested to my friends that we go there for mid-day drinks as that's where the stars would be staying. We got there, and I bought a round when suddenly, standing next to me at the bar was the one and only Tom T Hall. I struck up a conversation and we all had our photos taken with him. Seek and you will find, that's been my motto!

Later, we saw two old men sitting in the hotel and one of my friends, Peter Russell, said he knew them and began talking to them. We looked on amazed as he was talking to Tommy Overstreet and Johnny Russell who were country singers and the latter a songwriter best known for 'Act Naturally' which was made famous by Buck Owens. We were having a fantastic time and as a receptionist walked past I asked if he could get us a car to the festival. A short while afterwards a porter came up and told us our limousine was waiting outside!

They'd obviously taken us for part of the entourage and the driver asked if we wanted to be taken to the stage door. I said to drop us off at a burger bar and we'd make our own way from there!

I took Barbara to another country music festival in Grantham, in a place called Strumpshaw, where Margaret Thatcher was born. We had a hotel for the weekend and went with some friends. Another friend, Billy Worral, had a caravan at the site where we based ourselves during the day. We got there around eleven in the morning and sat by the van having a drink and looking forward to watching the country music singers, though none were very famous. It was a lovely sunny day, so I decided to go for a walk. I got to a beer stall and decided to stop for one and got chatting to a man standing next to me at the bar. He was American and told me he was on stage the following morning. His name was Bobby Lee Springfield and he'd just made a record called 'Chain Gang'. After a few more beers I invited him back to the caravan and introduced him to my friends. He stayed for about six hours, talking about music and drinking our beer. After he'd had quite a few he told me he was adopted as a child and his real mother and father were Marilyn Monroe and John F Kennedy! The following morning, midway through a song Bobby stopped to say hi to me before carrying on. A great end to a lovely weekend.

Soon after returning to Tilbury, Barbara put her house on the market and it quickly sold. We decided to rent for a while until we could find the right property and settled on a three-bedroomed place in London Road, Grays. The agent was David Cope of Copes Estate Agents and I got to know him, telling him I was going to work for myself as a decorator once I'd finished the security job. He said he had a lot of work he could give me, so I quickly handed in my notice and started trading under the company name of 'In & Out Decorators and Office Cleaners'. Later, I added carpet cleaning to that. My main jobs were clearing out and re-painting flats that had been vacated by their tenants, as well as tidying up the gardens, all ready for the new tenants. I started working for a few other letting agencies and private landlords even having to change the locks when there were evictions. Some of the places were left in a real mess and they still wondered why they didn't get their deposits back. One, in East Tilbury, had a black ceiling and red walls like the house of Hell. I needed about three gallons of white paint to bring it back to its original state. After doing this nothing else would phase me!

We got settled in our new place although the road outside was very busy, particularly at weekends when people went to Lakeside, a very large shopping centre. We would also visit as we enjoyed the restaurants. On Sunday's I'd visit one of the many boot fairs looking for tools, paint brushes and the like. I also enjoyed chatting to the stallholders.

I went to a lot of record fairs as I was really into country music, mainly Johnny Cash, and managed to collect over three hundred of his albums, as part of a collection of well over a thousand country records. Fortunately for me, Barbara also liked country and her favourite artist being George Jones who was once married to Tammy Wynette, the queen of country who sadly passed away some time ago.

While at London Road we decided to get another cat to join Lucy, who we'd got when living in Tilbury. Sadly, by then we'd lost Tansy as she was old and became ill. We got our new addition from a pet shop just up the road, a dear little white kitten we named Tango, though I'm not sure why as she wasn't orange. She was only with us for a couple of weeks when she got diarrhoea and sickness and Barbara rushed her to the vets as I was at work, but she passed away whilst there. We were very sad, and a few weeks passed but we decided to get another cat and picked up Jake who was a smart looking black and white kitten. He developed similar symptoms after a few days, so we rushed again to the vets but happily this time everything was fine, and we had our dear Jake for another twenty years.

We were still looking for another place and it needed to be away from a busy road for the sake of the cats. The traffic was bad and one morning it was brought to a standstill. Around six-thirty in the morning we heard a loud bang from right outside our front window and when we looked out a car had crashed into the front wall of a house a few doors up from us. The driver was out of the car and I saw him throw a beer bottle into a nearby hedge. The police arrived, and I told them the driver was drunk which they replied that they could see for themselves! I also told them where they could find the evidence. Therefore, we wanted to move somewhere new.

Not long afterwards we got our mortgage in place and found a house in Kent Road, Grays. The first thing we needed to do was sort the kitchen out as the cupboard doors were falling off and there was no oven. We got a new kitchen from MFI and I finished off the tiling and painting. Barbara was happy now as we'd been living off takeaways for about a month and must have had every Chinese dish on the menu. The next job was the garden which was in a terrible state. I laid a new patio and bought turfs for the lawn. It all took about two months as I was still working so it was very tiring but worth it in the end. Our neighbours each side were two men who each lived alone, George and Mick. George would play his train videos on a Sunday morning and you could hear the whistles. He loved everything about them.

Most of the houses in the road had been built in the early nineteen hundreds but varied in style. You could almost imagine the horses and carts down there years ago. Over the back was a large allotment that had been left to local people many years ago. Along the other side of the allotments was Whitehall Lane with similar houses and a few bungalows, one of which the Krays apparently used to visit back in the sixties.

The work at this time wasn't steady but it was a new start and I had to persevere. I got a few jobs over in Chigwell and Ilford for a man called Mr Mamelok, who owned many properties in these areas. I also did some work for his daughter Cathy who was married to the politician, James Brokenshire, and lived in Debden in Essex. I remember my first job for Mr Mamelok was a small hotel in South Woodford that he'd extended from twelve rooms to twenty and sold off years later for a tidy sum. He did most of the work himself, putting in sinks, plumbing and electricity so all I needed to do was plaster and paint. He was very hands-on and a nice man to work for.

Whilst I was working in Ilford a few people would see the van and ask me to do some work for them, but I had to be a bit choosy as most wanted it done for next to nothing. I remember starting a job for a man who was a Russian Jew who wanted me to paint a room in his house. When I arrived and brought my ladder through there was an old lady sitting in one corner. I said to the man that she would have to go before I could continue but he insisted she had to stay there. I left there and then as I couldn't continue working with her staring at me all day!

I also did some work for a man called Dr Gay who lived with his family in Manor Road. He also had a holiday let in Brighton that I did some painting work on. I even got as far as Selsey Bill on the south coast of England for another client.

Back in Grays I got a call from a woman who wanted me to paint her kitchen and lounge. We agreed a price and I said it would take two days to complete. I called her Mrs Dust as when I arrived she asked where I was going to put the kitchen furniture and when I looked I could only see cupboards and worktops. I realised she wanted me to move these out as she said there was dust behind them. I thought she was joking at first but apparently not, so I said she'd need a team of plumbers and electricians to do all of that! I ended up just doing the decorating which she was pleased with, but I never went back there.

By now I had another decorator working with me. I explained there would be some days I couldn't give him work and he was fine with it. But it was handy having someone who could carry on when I went on holiday. We had some nice times away to places such as Cyprus with our friends Dave and Francis and their daughter Victoria, as well as Barbara's daughter Keeley. Our neighbour Eileen looked after the cats and it was great to get away after the hectic year we'd had.

Barbara's dad, Bill lived in a nice bungalow in Hornchurch with his second wife Anne, as Barbara's mum had passed away in 1977. We would visit every fortnight and around this time Bill wasn't in the best of health, so we made sure we kept a regular check along with Barbara's brother Peter and his wife Christine who lived in Lydden, near Dover. We'd booked to go to Menorca and though it was a hotel in the middle of nowhere we didn't mind. On the holiday we discussed getting married as we wanted to Bill to see it and as soon as we got home we went to tell them the news. They were delighted so we booked it for six weeks later. Sadly, Bill passed away two weeks before the ceremony and we asked Anne if she wanted us to postpone but she said no, and that Bill would have wanted it to go ahead.

So, we booked a pub called the Dog and Partridge in Kelvedon Hatch for the meal afterwards and got married at Grays Registry Office. The weather was good, and everyone enjoyed the day. We had a lovely surprise as Peter and Chris had booked the four of us into a lovely hotel in the Cotswolds and afterwards we spent a few more days with them at their home.

Chapter Seventeen

Work, Rest and Play

I took a call one day from a woman called Mrs Roxburgh, asking if I wanted to do some painting work. She was director of Hackney Independent Learning Team, or HILT for short. They were an organisation that housed people with special needs and mental health problems. Perhaps she'd heard about my caring nature!

I agreed to go and meet her and the staff. Some people were housed in a single complex and others shared houses around Hackney. Myself and an assistant started working on one of the houses and soon learned some valuable lessons. One day I made the mistake of leaving my lunch in the kitchen and when I returned for it one of the tenants was just finishing it off, as they were told that they could eat anything left in the kitchen. On another occasion I put my overalls on and started working when one of the staff said it would be quiet as they were going to Southend for the day. I watched them leave on the coach and as it started to pull away I noticed a young woman wearing a jumper remarkably like the one I'd had on earlier. She'd obviously taken a liking to it and it took the carers ages to get it back from her. I did say she could keep it, but they insisted she return it as otherwise it would send out the wrong message to her.

One morning I went into the kitchen to make a cup of tea. The tenants, or 'service users' as they were known were seated at a round table, drawing. I was told by the staff to finish my tea and make myself scarce as an independent assessment team were coming in to interview the service users. No sooner had she said this when one of the assessment team walked in, made a bee-line for me, held my hand and asked my name. I realised straight away what was occurring, so I told her it was James. She asked how long I'd been there and I said about four months. She then asked if I liked it here and I replied that it was ok. The conversation was flowing now, and she enquired to whether I was friends with anyone, so I put on a sad face and told her I talked to them, but they didn't talk to me. She asked me why I didn't have a colouring book and pens like the others. I'd strung this out long enough, so I said it's because I'm the decorator.

She dropped my hand and couldn't get back to her team quickly enough! When I told Barbara later she was in fits of giggles and said it could only happen to me.

The part of Hackney I worked in had a lot of Orthodox Jews living there, with their black clothes and distinctive black hats. The young boys dressed the same way and had ringlets down the sides of their faces. This fascinated me.

HILT had a special unit near the junction of Lea Bridge Road that housed service users with what some would term serious mental health problems and so some of the staff were working one-to-one with them. The unit was usually in lockdown and hard to get out of, and you needed to be on the ball when working there as the moment you put your mobile phone down anywhere, you'd end up finding it later in one of the toilet bowls. I found it quite stressful working there, but the pay made up for it. I would make sure I was always polite and friendly, as these people needed a smile from time to time. Though I did get told off one day for bringing in a teddy bear for a woman called Linda who was in a wheelchair who had lots of bears in her room. But I was just being me. I had been working at HILT for around a year and was about to get another call that would make me very happy, ironically from a woman called Mrs Jolly!

Jo Jolly lived in Enfield with her husband Tim and daughter Sarah. She asked if I'd do some decorating work at her house and though we thought it would be a long journey for me, Barbara and I agreed to see how it went. I carried on for a while with the letting agency work, but it wasn't really making much money, so I decided to buy a carpet-cleaning machine and went on a user's course. This would help bring in some extra cash.

Jo Jolly called back to see if I wanted the work and as it was a nice, sunny day I drove over to the house. It was probably one of the biggest houses I've ever seen or been inside. They wanted the stairs, passage and landing decorated and started soon afterwards. When I was there I noticed a grey Mazda 303 on the driveway that never seemed to move and mentioned this to Jo. She said she was selling it as they had a new one and I asked for first refusal. I bought it soon afterwards and got a real bargain. When they came to drop it off, Jo and her husband came into our house and asked where all our clutter was. I said it was in the cupboards! I had the car for twelve years and it always passed its MOT, but then again it wasn't used a lot as I also had my van.

When I finished the job, Jo asked if I'd like to do some work at 'Living Space' in Marsh Hill, Hackney. This was a place for people with learning disabilities who had rooms to live in, within a controlled environment. She said a lot of the previous painters had been light-fingered and wanted someone reliable. She gave me all the details of the work that needed doing and when I got home that evening I needed to sit and take it all in. I told Barbara to go and treat herself as things were looking up. The amount of jobs and money on offer was much more than I'd been used to in this line of work.

The aim was to paint a room each day, with the ceiling, walls, undercoating and top-coating, and all woodwork included. I had to start at eight in the morning and be finished by three in the afternoon, so the tenants could move back in. I got used to the pace of it after a while although sometimes couldn't finish until about four. It was different to HILT as you could talk to the tenants, but we had to be careful so if anyone was working for me I made sure they didn't leave their paint pots around. We also had to make sure none of the tenants mistook the white spirit for lemonade! We treated everyone with respect and always friendly but did need to keep our eyes open as some of the workmen were a little dodgy and would lift things like Henry Hoovers if they got the chance.

Back at Kent Road we now had the house to ourselves as Paul had his own place and was working in the Civil Service, and Keeley was off at Camp America. She had always been into athletics and ran for her local club.

I got a call one day from Mrs Brokenshire asking if I'd decorate a house in Hornchurch that they were soon to move into. Her husband had left his job as a lawyer after being elected as the local MP. The first thing was to get rid of the old carpets and fitted wardrobes, but although the carpets went to the dump, the wardrobes ended up in our back bedroom. We got the job done and moved on to working back at Living Space, as well as doing occasional gardening work for Jo Jolly. It made a nice change to use a lawnmower instead of a paintbrush.

We had another holiday with our friends, this time in Albufeira, Portugal where we'd booked a villa with a pool. Our good friend and neighbour Eileen tended the cats. She and her husband Harry sometimes came over for a drink and were very good to us all the time we lived there. I even found out that one of their lodgers from years ago was a man called Lew Hardy, a merchant seaman and then a mercenary soldier. I couldn't believe it as he'd taken me under his wing years ago when I first started on the voyages to Australia. He was a good friend and a tough cookie, with eyes that said, 'don't mess with me'. In a bar one evening in Sydney we were chatting to a woman and her husband suddenly came over in a bad mood and started having a go at us for talking to his wife. Lew simply put his hand under the man's chin and lifted him off the floor. The husband swiftly apologised and returned to where he'd been sitting without another word. Sadly, Lew passed on a few years ago but I remember the good times and drinks we had.

We had a lovely time in Portugal with our friends Dave and Francis; their daughter Victoria and her husband, Gary. Our villa was lovely and only a short walk from the beach and restaurants. We would buy rolls, meat and salad for our lunch then go out for our evening meals. The walk back to our villa was along a long lane that had no lighting and we'd often see a man with one arm standing near our place, which spooked us quite a bit and we couldn't get the key in the door quickly enough. One night we were in the kitchen, wondering about who this man was and Gary, who'd excused himself to go off to the loo, went outside and put his arm through the open window, making groaning noises. We all stated screaming and shouting but it was funny. After all, what could a one-armed man do against all of us! We saw the man again a few days later selling fish out of a small open truck.

We spent a lot of time relaxing around the pool, drinking and reading, and re-charging our batteries. One thing about our holidays was that we'd always adopt a cat that hung around nearby, and Barbara would buy cat food in the local shops for them.

I never enjoyed coming home after a holiday. The grass needed cutting and there was shopping to be done. But we did enjoy catching up on the gossip from the street, as there were always curtain twitchers who knew.

was going on. I admit to doing it myself when there was a good row outside. The road was becoming increasingly crowded with cars and there was no guarantee of getting parked outside your house after you'd gone out. I suppose I didn't help, having a car and a van. Some of the parking was terrible too, with people taking up more than one space with just one car, and an elderly woman who lived a few doors away we named Mrs Crash because she must have bumped into every car in the street. One day I suggested she gave up driving after nearly missing my car and getting in such a state I had to park her car for her but insisted it was only parking she had problems with. She even crashed into the churchyard wall once but paid for the damage.

Working for Living Space was like painting the Forth Bridge as you moved from the complex to the houses and back to the complex again. Whenever someone moved into one of the rooms they could choose the colour and I then went in to do the work. One of the complexes which housed about twenty people was run by a man called David Walls who I got on well with. One of the people who lived there was called George and always made a bee-line for me. George was a man of the road, or a tramp if you like and a real character around Hackney. A small man with long hear and a beard, he used his room to sleep but would go out all day and would always ask me "got a cigarette guvnor?" or "got money for a cup of tea guvnor?" and when I gave him something he'd always reply, "God bless you guvnor".

Another resident whose name I can't recall would get a train to the West End, taking his tapes and would play music and dance in front of people lining up to see a show. He would often get a fair bit of money but sadly one time he was mugged and ended up in hospital and was never the same afterwards.

Chapter Eighteen

More Work, Rest and Play

It's now 2006. Keeley has moved to a house in Grays and has a baby on the way. She works in London and her boyfriend, Dave, is an Industrial Electrician. We miss the company but get to see them often. It gave us more time for holidays, so we booked a short break with our friends, to Rome. We would miss the wedding of Prince Charles and Camilla Parker-Bowles but that didn't really worry us!

What did worry us was that the Pope had recently died and was being buried on the day our plane landed. On the day, they announced that all flights were being diverted so we ended up eighty miles away and had to pay for a coach back to the city. It was strange because we expected to find huge crowds, but it was deserted. It also rained the entire time we were there, so the trip was a bit of a washout. But we did have a good time at the Colosseum.

Back home I'd joined the digital revolution and got back in touch with some old friends via Facebook. I also joined ebay and started buying a few things off the site. One day I noticed a pair of size twelve trainers for just over two pounds and thought they'd do me well for work as I was always getting paint over my good shoes. So, I sent the money across and forgot all about it.

I'd cut my work down a bit by now but kept busy visiting Barbara's step-mum, helping with shopping and doing any odd-jobs. One Saturday morning Barbara brought the post in, smiling, and handed me a couple of letters and a small box. I wondered what the box contained and soon discovered it was my trainers, but they were size twelve for babies. It gave everyone in the family a good laugh and learned to be more careful on ebay!

Working for Living Space I visited another of their secure units in Clarence Road where I had to do mostly night-work, so the paint was dry by the time everyone came in for their breakfast. I also started working at a house with six residents. The staff member gave me my parking permit and told me where to park. I went outside and just to be certain I asked a parking attendant where I should put my car, as I showed him my pass. He showed me, and I thanked him, but remembered to take a note of his number in case there were any problems. Which there were. I finished work and returned to the car to find a parking ticket on the windscreen. I returned the ticket with a letter explaining that I had a pass and had been shown where to park by the attendant, giving his number for reference. I added that I'd see them in court and charge any expenses to them. I got a letter back stating that I didn't need to pay the fine but there was no apology, just informing me not to do it again. Is it any wonder we love traffic wardens?

My van was yellow, with red writing on the side and stood out a mile. One afternoon I was travelling home through Ilford when I noticed congestion ahead so went down a side road to avoid it as I was in a hurry. I got to the corner and saw a hearse go by. I pulled out behind it and immediately realised my mistake as I was now part of the procession and couldn't get out of it. It was like a scene from Only Fools and Horses as my yellow van crawled along amongst the hearse and black cars. I was stuck there for about fifteen minutes and people were looking and laughing. Barbara also had a good laugh when I told her later. As she said, "only you"!

Towards the end of the tax year, Living Space were careful with their budget, so work slowed down a bit, but would soon pick up after April. I took advantage of this by doing some small jobs that came in, and Mr Mamelok was always handy for this as I could give him a call and he'd have some work for me. It was also a good time to take another holiday, so Barbara and I booked to go to America to visit the Grand Canyon and Las Vegas. It turned out to be one of the best trips we ever had. We got a flight to Los Angeles and a coach to Knotts Berry Farm where we stayed overnight, then on to Laughlin, Nevada where our hotel was. The place was lively at night with lots of casinos and each hotel having about five hundred rooms.

When we left Knotts Berry Farm our suitcases were lined up outside the hotel, ready for the coach to arrive. But when it did, the driver backed up to the cases and the back wheel crushed a corner of the one on the end. Yes, you guessed it. Our case.

Our first day trip was to Hollywood and we visited the Walk of Fame as well as the many shops where we looked for gifts to take home. The following day we went to Oatman, Arizona which was once a thriving mining town during the gold rush, but now just a ghost town. Located there was the Durlin Hotel where Clark Gable and Carole Lombard spent their wedding night in 1939. The remaining town folk staged a gun fight for us and we had a drink in the saloon bars. We also went down a mine in one of the small trains which topped off a good day out.

The meals in America were a new experience for us as they were so big, and I don't think we ever finished one, but I loved the steaks and the endless coffee refills. On the day of the Grand Canyon trip it was nice and sunny, so some people booked helicopter rides. Our coach dropped us off at a vantage point with a great view of the canyon and there was a large bar where we went in for a drink. After about an hour we ventured back outside and couldn't believe our eyes as it was now covered in snow, about two feet deep. Even the guides said they'd never seen anything like it before and unfortunately all the helicopter rides had to be cancelled. On the way back, we stopped at the Hoover Dam and a souvenir shop along Route 66 where we bought a replacement for our damaged suitcase as well as a vanity case and holdall, with 'Route 66' plastered all over them.

Our last day was a visit to Las Vegas and there was a lot to take in, with all the chapels, crazy outfits and pampered dogs with their owners. We noticed a shopping mall and wanted to get Keeley something for the baby. We were looking through what we thought was a children's clothing and shoe shop but couldn't understand why the baby shoes were all so wide. We called an assistant to ask and she told us they were for the bears. So, we left and as we got outside, noticed the shop was called 'Bear Necessities'. How embarrassing!

We had to visit a couple of the famous hotels and casinos, and we were shocked by the people at the machines with their credit cards inserted by a chain.

It was an enjoyable trip and we managed to get compensation for our ruined suitcase, after a few arguments.

Like most people, I never enjoy coming back and getting into work again, but I soon got into the swing of things. Living Space would email the work they wanted doing so I could go and choose the colour paint they'd picked. I was still earning well and after Barbara told me I'd be 71 before the mortgage was paid off I decided to investigate how much was left. We were told it was around eleven thousand pounds and we had just about enough to phone the Building Society and pay it off, which was a great feeling.

Soon after this, Keeley gave birth to a healthy boy named Sam. Our first grandson, as we had two grand-daughters, Charlotte and Sophie, from Paul's side. The next couple of years passed uneventfully until April 2008 when Barbara went in for a routine mammogram and it was discovered she had a lump in her breast. She had a biopsy which confirmed it was cancerous, and an MRI to check there were no further lumps. Happily, there weren't so a lumpectomy was carried out on 5th June, which was Sam's second birthday. It all went well, and the regular checks were so far so good, and after all the trauma we decided another holiday was well deserved. So, we booked a trip along the River Nile for later in the year.

The time arrived, and we flew to Luxor, joining our ship there. It was a small vessel holding about fifty passengers. The crew were mostly Nubian, taken from the tribes along the river. Breakfast consisted of a buffet of bread, eggs, spam, cakes and pots of jam and dinner was usually chicken or bully beef with mash or their version of roast potatoes which were always hard. We went on some excursions ashore and the Egyptian people always seemed to be in your face wanting tips for everything, and if you bought anything they were very slow in giving your change. We did all the usual sites such as the Valley of the Kings, Tutankhamun's Tomb and the Tomb of Ramses VI, as well as camel trekking. All enjoyable but very hot. Halfway along our cruise we moored up to take a boat trip to Lord Kitchener's Island, to see the botanical gardens. As we sailed there, a boatload of local boys came alongside singing 'row row row the boat' and as a laugh I shouted to them in Japanese, so they sang in Japanese! Someone else shouted in German so they sang a German version, and so on. We didn't mind giving them some money as they'd given us a good laugh.

Every evening on the cruise there would be a show, with dancers in full Egyptian dress. One of the dancers would spin round fast on the spot for around two minutes then stop and just walk offstage normally.

Although the menu on the boat consisted of little other than chicken, when we were ashore we never saw any in the markets or elsewhere. Unfortunately, a few passengers, including me, were ill with food poisoning. One elderly lady was on a drip for a couple of days but managed to recover by the time we got to Aswan. The cruise came to an end and as we were leaving the boat, Barbara noticed all the pots and pans being washed in the Nile, which is all we needed to see and explained the illnesses on board. Our coach was late picking us up and got a puncture a few miles from the airport, so to get there in time we'd have to move to one side of the coach, so he could finish the journey. I don't think that would have happened in England. It was a lovely trip in some respects, but never again!

We were back home and glad to see our cats had been well looked after again by our lovely neighbours. We never sent them to a cattery as they looked so unloved when you picked them up. I had a job soon after returning, to evict a woman from Grays who hadn't paid her rent. I accompanied the Bailiff who told her she had two hours to leave. She tried every trick in the book to get out of it but there was a court order, so she had to go. I ended up helping her to remove all her possessions before changing the locks and going back to redecorate. It was sad to see but had to be done.

We would often pop into Grays town centre of a weekend to do some shopping. There were often buskers around playing the same old songs and a few times we saw Don Estelle in his khaki outfit and hat singing 'Whispering Grass' and selling his CDs. He did look a sorry sight and I think he passed away the following year.

One day I got the bad news that Living Space was to be taken over by a Housing Association. It was happening more and more, so I knew it was on the cards, but Jo Jolly gave me work right up to the point they were taken over and I can't thank her enough for that. She decided it was the right point to retire and so did I. I visited all the residents before I left, to say goodbye. They'd become like a family to me and I still wonder how they are all getting along.

Now I had time to do a few jobs around the house that I'd been putting off and we had more time to babysit our grandson Sam. I kept my hand in a little bit doing the odd job for Mr Mamelok.

Soon after I hung up my paintbrush, my daughter Jane invited us to their villa in Majorca, where they had a time-share. It was a large place next to a golf course in the middle of nowhere. Jane and Simon, her husband, liked to go there just to chill out and we would often cook our own meals rather than going out. They still went down well with a couple of bottles of wine. We decided to do our own version of the programme 'Come Dine with Me' as competing couples and had to pick the best meal. They were all nice, but Simon decided on Vodka Melon for dessert. He left a whole bottle soaking into the melon and unfortunately it only seemed to soak into one part. Out of all of us, Barbara was the one who drank the least, so guess who got the piece with all the vodka! I did poached pear in red wine and if I say so myself, it was delicious. Although we'd had a good laugh at Barbara's expense with the melon we decided to call it a draw. Now every time the programme comes on the telly it reminds us of this holiday. Sadly, it was to be one of our last major holidays as ill health was around the corner for both of us.

Chapter Nineteen

Funerals, Trouble from Asda and Fame at Last

In September 2008 I had a telephone call from my Dad's wife Betty, telling me he was in a council run nursing home and had been unwell for some time, suffering from dementia. Before he was in the home he'd often go on walkabouts and be brought home by the police. Betty and my dad had lived in a two-bedroomed flat in a warden-controlled complex in Hainault. He often enjoyed walks then, mainly to the bookies.

Although I hadn't spoken to him for many years I told Betty I'd visit and when I got there he asked who I was. I told him I was Jimmy and he asked if I was from Canning Town. I replied that I was as all the family had been from around there. Then he just went to sleep. I stayed for about half an hour while he slept and the next time I went he didn't remember me from the previous visit. Shortly afterwards Betty called to say he'd been taken to hospital, so we collected her and went straight there. When we arrived, he was in a deep sleep and unresponsive. We spoke to the doctor who told us to expect the worst, so we stayed for as long as we could but left at the end of the day. We got home and there was a call soon after to say he had passed away. The funeral was a few weeks later and on the day, it was freezing cold. I got out of the funeral car and saw my cousin George with some friends of the family. I had on a black suit and overcoat and walked over to say hello. George looked very surprised before realising who I was. He'd initially thought I was from the funeral company.

The vicar spoke of my dad's marriage to Betty and said something that shocked everyone apart from immediate family. He told the congregation that in thirty years of marriage he'd not once made Betty a cup of tea. My father was the sort of man that believed women were put on the earth to clean, cook and shop. Whenever they went shopping together he would stay outside in the car and always checked up if she got home late. Rest in peace dad, but you never treated women properly.

My father was buried in the East London Cemetery with his first wife, my mum Anne. After the funeral Barbara and I would visit Betty often, along with her own daughter Rita who would make the long trip from Wickford twice a week. Betty had a lot of friends on the complex so would only leave to go shopping with Rita. After he passed away, Betty started finding money he'd hidden away around the flat. Not a great deal, just the odd ten or twenty-pound note, probably for a trip to the betting shop. We continued to visit Betty for a couple of years as she wasn't in the best of health, suffering from back pain and poor eyesight, but she was always in good spirits, talking of the old days and having a giggle. She could also hold a good tune on the mouth organ!

Sadly, one day we received a call from Rita to say that Betty had passed away. It was a shock despite knowing it would happen eventually, as she was 98. On the day of the funeral there were a lot of people and though I was sad I couldn't help noticing my sister June's ex-husband paying his last respects. I couldn't believe he'd turned up in jeans and a donkey jacket! Betty was cremated at Forest Park Crematorium in Hainault, a stones throw away from where I'd been brought up. It was a shame we weren't in their lives when they were married but family rifts happen.

One afternoon soon after this we were sitting in our lounge when we saw an Asda truck drive slowly past our house, then heard the bleeps that meant it was reversing. Suddenly, we saw my Mazda jolt and I went out to find the driver had clipped the back of the car resulting in the back light smashing and a few dents in the side. The woman who'd being driving admitted responsibility and fortunately we had a witness so exchanged insurance details. The driver said Asda would quickly pay up, so I got on to my insurance company and they told me to write directly to Asda to move things along. I was also told I couldn't drive the car in its current condition and put me in touch with a car hire firm. I called them to make arrangements and the following evening they arrived with a top of the range Jaguar that I couldn't wait to take for a spin. The accident happened in January and though I sent the letter and followed up with several calls, there was no response over the next few months. It got to August and I began to worry in case the insurance would make me pay for the hire car, so I found the details for Asda Head Office and wrote to the Director. I explained that I'd had the hire car for several months and was still waiting to hear back about my claim. I even threatened to go to the press. It seemed to do the trick as an assessor came to the house a few days later and shortly after this I was offered three hundred and fifty pounds for the damage. I accepted this, and the hire firm came back for the Jaguar. I asked them what they were planning to charge Asda and they told me it would be nearly ten thousand pounds!

I managed to get the work done for fifty pounds and made sure I always stayed clear of Asda lorries after this. The Mazda was eighteen years old but drove well, so I sold it for two hundred and fifty pounds which wasn't bad considering Jo Jolly had let me have it for two hundred. By now, Keeley had given birth to a second beautiful baby boy called Jack, so we were proud grandparents of two boys and two girls, and all one big happy family.

When I retired life became easier, not having to get up early and go to work on cold winter mornings, though I'd still be up early and down to the local newsagents for the morning paper. I heard that one of our neighbours, Monty, was going to be the subject of a television makeover programme called 'You Deserve this House' presented by Amanda Lamb. Monty did a lot of good work in the local community with young adults and all she knew is that her company had sent her on a two-day spa break as a reward for her had work. In the meantime, there were two days to transform her kitchen, bedroom and bathroom so a team of workmen were brought in and a mobile catering van set up nearby. The producers asked if they could store the new furniture in our front garden and to use our loo now and again if the workmen had too much tea. We were fine about this and they came in to put sheets all over the stairs and passage, so the carpets wouldn't get damaged or dirty.

As you can imagine there was a lot of noise as the old kitchen was ripped out and the new furniture started going in. Amanda Lamb came in a few times to chat and use the facilities and was very nice to us. We were sitting down to dinner on the first evening, enjoying a bottle of wine and relaxing before the England football international when there was a knock at the door. I answered it and the producer was standing there. He said one of the tilers had left early and everything needed to be finished by lunchtime the next day. He'd been told by a neighbour that I could turn my hand to most things and asked if I'd help to do some tiling in the kitchen. Reluctantly I agreed, though I'd be getting my fifteen minutes of fame. The last time I'd been in the public eye was way back when the Tower Bridge walkways opened, and I was on the front page of the Evening Standard. They asked if I wanted to pay but I said no. The man who was meant to do it was one of the people Monty had helped but he had to go because it was his son's birthday. So, from eight until eleven that night I was tiling instead of relaxing and watching the football.

The next day I was asked to go back to do the grouting. In fact, the only thing I didn't do was tile around the plugs as I didn't have a cutter. Eventually the tiler came back and finished the work off, and I was thanked by the team for stepping in, as well as opening our house to the crew. The homecoming for Monty was that afternoon and everyone crowded into our lounge as Amanda Lamb met her outside the front gate to break the surprise. Monty was obviously delighted and as she came back out we were all standing outside clapping and cheering. She thanked everyone and gave me a big hug. Although I'd done most of the tiling I didn't get mentioned on the closing credits, but I'd enjoyed it and done a good job considering I was half drunk on the first night. After the programme aired I'm sure I got a few people pointing and whispering when I went out shopping.

Chapter Twenty

Cancer, Heart Attack and a Visit from Hasnat Khan

Soon after my television fame I had to go for my yearly blood test at Orsett Hospital. I was at home the following morning when I received a call from the GP's receptionist informing me I had to go and see the doctor. I went along the same day to be told my PSA levels were very high and I was being referred to Basildon Hospital.

When I got there, I had to undergo further tests and unfortunately the results were concerning so I had to go to Southend Hospital for even more tests and a biopsy that couldn't be done at Basildon. The results came back a week later, showing I had prostate cancer. The only good news was that they'd caught it early, and I was given the choice of having the prostate removed or radiation treatment. I talked it over with Barbara and decided it would be best to have the operation. Around this time, our family from Australia, Jean and Bill had flown over for six weeks to visit Anne and so I lent them my car for the duration as I knew I wouldn't be able to drive it.

It was only a week or so later that I was admitted to Southend Hospital for the operation. I was told it was successful and would be allowed to go home after a few days. I had lots of visitors and Jean and Bill picked me up in my car when it was time to go. When I got home I had to wear a catheter for two weeks and then pads after it had been removed in case there were any problems with my bladder. Unfortunately, there were, and these continued up until 2016 when I had another operation at University College Hospital in London, to insert a surgical sling which would stop any more leaks.

When I woke from the second operation I had another catheter which was removed after two days and the nurses had to monitor my bladder control. I left the hospital wearing pads again but by now I had proper control over my bladder and was able to discard them quickly afterwards. To this day I've not had any more problems with it and I feel very lucky to have had the procedure done so quickly at the only hospital that carries out that type of operation.

But back to 2013. We wanted to put the previous year behind us and spend quality time babysitting, doing our usual things and continuing to visit Barbara's step-mum, Anne every weekend. She was finding it harder to get out and about but was quite content at home and got regular visits from her friend Tilly who lived up the road. We'd go for her shopping and I'd do some odd jobs around her bungalow. One Saturday morning we were getting ready for our visit when I started to feel pains in my chest and my arms really ached. I told Barbara and we went off to the medical centre in Grays. As I was waiting to see the doctor the pain was getting worse and after an hour I was called in, near to tears with the pain and trauma. She checked me over and put me on an ECG monitor. Then she gave me some aspirin and a letter referring me to Basildon Hospital. I had to get the bus there straight away, so we started walking back to the house to get my bus pass. Halfway there I started to feel more pain and realised I was having a heart attack but didn't want to frighten Barbara, so I just walked a bit quicker and held my hands to my chest.

Barbara phoned Keeley who rushed us over there and soon had me on a trolley. The doctor confirmed I'd had a heart attack and I told him I knew, and they were going to send me on the bus! I didn't know at the time, but I was going to be in hospital for five weeks. First, I was sent to a general ward where they did lots of tests and after two weeks I was given an Angiogram which allows the doctor to see inside your coronary arteries and find out how severe any narrow areas were. From this diagnosis they were able to tell me I was going to have a quadruple bypass. Another week later I was taken to the Cardiothoracic Unit for more tests, including blowing into a tube so they could assess the force of the air and determine how they would set up the heart support machine after the operation.

The day before the op I was told to shave all over and given a new gown. I was allowed visitors in the afternoon and was quite tearful when they left. I gave Barbara a big hug before she went. The surgeon was Mr Nikolaos Charokopos, who came to see me in the evening, followed by the anaesthetist who informed me there was a risk of death, but I should be ok! The last visit was from the Hospital Chaplain who wanted to say a prayer, but it was the last person I wanted to see. I just wanted to talk with Barbara.

The next morning, I was ready to go, and it was a five-hour operation, then straight into intensive care. That evening Barbara and Keeley came to visit, and I think it was a bit of a shock to see me hooked up to all these machines. Later, Barbara told me they were both very upset. I was only half conscious but under strict instruction from the nurse to keep breathing! I was taken off the machines around midnight but stayed in intensive care until the following afternoon, then brought back to the ward where I had a visit from another surgeon called Mr Hasnat Khan, who was once the boyfriend of Princess Diana. We had a chat about my condition and how I should progress in the future. The unit I was on was monitored so only family could visit due to the risk of infection. I can't say I enjoyed my stay, but the nurses were all very good and it was a caring place to be.

I was allowed home after another eight days and had to attend rehabilitation classes for another couple of weeks, to build up my strength. Then plenty of rest. While all this was going on Barbara had health issues of her own, with doctors and hospital visits. It seemed to take over our lives at the time, and Barbara ended up having a major operation the following year. In the meantime, I was still having routine checks for the prostate removal at Southend Hospital and the PSA levels were fine, but the doctor recommended a tablet which would help with the bladder problems. If I'd known what would happen I'd never have taken them! I'd just been for a routine blood test and later that morning had a call from the doctor asking me to go to the surgery straight away. When I got there, he said my blood count was so low it was a wonder I was still walking. He gave me a letter and told me to go straight to the hospital. I was admitted straight away, but still never got an Ambulance!

I was there for three days whilst they tried to sort out the problem, and after some prompting allowed me to go home on the Sunday, but that I had to be back first thing the next day. I had every type of test going while I was in there and the eventual outcome was the tablets I'd been given had affected my liver, so I stopped taking them immediately and after two more days I was discharged.

By now I was well and truly sick of hospitals and must hold the record for being in every ward in Basildon except the labour one. Things were fine for a time, but we got some bad news concerning Anne who'd been unwell for some time and it was discovered she had cancer of the inner ear. The doctors said it could be treated with radiotherapy and this would give her a chance of a few more good years, but she didn't like the mask that was fitted while undergoing the treatment and didn't want to go backwards and forwards to the hospital every day for weeks on end. After a lot of persuasion, she agreed to go twice a week, but it wasn't enough. Eventually she went into a hospice and sadly passed away. We both still remember her sitting in her chair in the corner of the living room, in the bungalow she loved so much.

We had by now decided to put our house on the market as we were fed up with the inconsiderate parking, and most of the neighbours we knew were also moving on. We got a buyer very quickly but had to pull out as we couldn't find anywhere we liked. After that we had a lot of viewers, mostly foreign, offering silly money and trying to barter you down like it's a boot sale. We were right to hang on as we eventually sold for five thousand over the original asking price. Our next house was in Chadwell St Mary, about four miles from where we lived before. It had three bedrooms and a driveway and garage, so I didn't have to worry about parking any more. It would be a bit of a project, but I had time now our hospital visits were less frequent. We missed going to Hornchurch to visit Anne but had our hands full babysitting, though we love it. All our grandchildren bring us lots of joy. We're pleased that they've been brought up in a swearing-free environment and you'll have noticed this book is virtually free of swearwords as hopefully my grandchildren are going to read it at some point.

Epilogue

The Boy from Hainault

In March 2016 we moved into our new home. There's plenty of work to do but I can do most of it, as its mainly painting and decorating. When we moved in the bathroom was separated from the toilet so that was the first thing to be changed, but we had to get the builders in for that one.

It took about three weeks to get that done but afterwards it was plain sailing. The woman who we bought from said her husband died a few years ago and she couldn't bear to go into the garage to clear it out, so I told her to leave it. There were tools galore, so I kept some and did a few car boot sales and went on Gumtree to sell the rest. It's now 2017 and I'm still clearing it out.

As I'm writing these final words we are looking to move again and downsize this time. Barbara's son Paul now lives in Norfolk and Keeley is still in Grays. We must think ahead as I won't be driving for much longer and we're not near any decent bus routes, especially if we need to make more visits to the hospital. Also, we don't want to be a burden to Keeley so we're looking for something a bit more suitable and our house is on the market. We've had a couple of offers near to the asking price, but we've not found anywhere we like so we're in no hurry to accept. The Estate Agents are confident it will go as we've spent a lot on it, and it's like a show-home. The Estate Agents have also told us we're known as LTBs, or 'last time buyers'!

I'm coming to the end of my story and my biggest thanks go to my wife Barbara who stood by me when times were tough, and to Jo Jolly for all the work she gave me, allowing us to have a good quality of life in the last years I was working.

I'm ending on a sad note. Some of you may remember seeing an item on the news about the baby, Charlie Gard, who was fighting for his life at Great Ormond Street Hospital, and the struggles of his parents with the health professionals. Charlie, if he had lived, would have been my third cousin. Rest in Peace Charlie.

To end my story, I'd like to say that although I've had a full life and travelled far and wide, I'll always be they boy from Hainault.

Printed in Great Britain
by Amazon

54315551R00054